CW01619063

Whose flexibility?

The costs and benefits of 'non-standard' working arrangements and contractual relations

Kate Purcell, Terence Hogarth and Claire Simm

The **Joseph Rowntree Foundation** has supported this project as part of its programme of research and innovative development projects, which it hopes will be of value to policy makers and practitioners. The facts presented and views expressed in this report are, however, those of the authors and not necessarily those of the Foundation.

Published for the Joseph Rowntree Foundation by YPS

ISBN 1 902633 37 7

Work and Opportunity Series No. 12

Cover design by Adkins Design

Prepared and printed by:
York Publishing Services Ltd
64 Hallfield Road
Layerthorpe
York YO31 7ZQ
Tel: 01904 430033; Fax: 01904 430868; E-mail: orders@yps.ymn.co.uk

Contents

Acknowledgements

The research undertaken in order to produce this report was funded by the Joseph Rowntree Foundation under their Work and Opportunity Programme. An Advisory Committee provided valuable guidance and feedback to the researchers. The research was undertaken at the Institute for Employment Research at the University of Warwick, by Kate Purcell, Terence Hogarth and Claire Simm. Kate Purcell is now Professor of Employment Studies at Bristol Business School in the University of the West of England. The authors are particularly grateful to Derek Williams (JRF Project Manager and Chair of the Advisory Committee), Professor Richard Brown (Professor Emeritus, Durham University), Dr Brendan Burchell (University of Cambridge), David Coats (Trades Union Congress), Gabrielle Cox (Greater Manchester Low Pay Unit), John McQueeney (Department of Trade and Industry) and Frank Wilkinson (University of Cambridge). John Stevens and Mike Emmott of the Institute for Personnel Development also provided useful feedback at particular stages of the project. Most of all, we would like to thank the managers, trade union officers, employees and other regional and national experts who allowed us to interview them in the course of the research and answered our questions with interest, patience and good humour. Maureen Garcia and Clare Jeffs provided excellent secretarial support.

Structure of the report

This report is based upon case study research undertaken between Autumn 1997 and Spring 1999. Its structure is as follows:

- Chapter 1 outlines the key issues relating to non-standard employment and labour force flexibility.
- Chapter 2 provides a summary of existing evidence relating to the deployment of flexible contracts of employment in the UK and presents an exploratory model developed to facilitate the cost–benefit analysis.
- Chapter 3 outlines the research design and methodology used, discussing the sectors and localities in which the research was undertaken.
- Evidence from the employer case studies is presented in Chapters 4 and 5 – relating, respectively to: the reasons *why* employers use flexible contracts of employment; and the costs and benefits that accrue to them.
- The costs and benefits of non-standard working arrangements and employment flexibility perceived by employees in the case study companies are presented in Chapter 6.
- Finally, Chapter 7 outlines the key findings and the implications of these for employers and policy-makers.

1 The key issues

Flexible employment

There has been considerable discussion in employment, policy and research arenas about employment flexibility and the increasingly wide variety of contractual relationships between employers and the people who work for them, either directly as employees or through an employment intermediary – who may be a sub-contracting firm or a labour supply agency. The widespread use of 'non-standard' employment patterns has increased throughout Europe in recent years, but is most established in the UK, where, of all EU member countries, employment is least regulated (Lindley, 1987; Crouch, 1996; Siebert, 1999). Such practices have been advocated as promoting numerical and labour cost flexibilities conducive to organisational efficiency and effectiveness (Atkinson and Meager, 1986; Corfield Wright, 1996), and have been perceived in a variety of recent European Commission White Papers as opening up new employment opportunities compatible with the reconciliation of work and family life (Moss, 1996). They have also been accused of leading to increasing employment insecurity, labour market polarisation and exploitation of the most disadvantaged groups (Dex and McCullough, 1995; Hutton, 1995).

At the end of the twentieth century, all the evidence from studies of the UK labour market suggests a widening income gap between individuals and households with access to secure employment and incomes and those whose labour market participation is more fragmented and tenuous (Joseph Rowntree Foundation, 1995; Gregg and Wadsworth, 1995; White, 1996; White and Forth, 1998). Women's economic activity has risen substantially, most notably part-time employment among mothers of dependent children under the age of five and among older women. Equality of opportunity in education and equal opportunities employment legislation encourage both sexes to regard access to employment and career development as a basic human right, but the uneasy reconciliation of work and family life in Britain has largely been achieved by means of a gender-segmented labour market where a substantial proportion of women work part-time or intermittently. Recently, however, two intriguing trends have developed. The first is an increasing polarisation of women in employment between those who work full-time and continuously over the life cycle (most often, those with relatively high skills and qualifications) and those who are confined to the secondary labour market and who are more likely to work part-time for a substantial part of their working lives (Hakim, 1996). The second is a substantial increase in male part-time employment (albeit from a low base). What both of these trends reveal is that employment opportunities – in particular, the way jobs are being constructed by employers – have been changing in the last decade.

In some contexts, contracts of employment which require willingness to vary working time arrangements and hours to accommodate fluctuations in product demand transfer some of the product market risk faced by employers onto the employee, by making their employment and wages more directly contingent upon work being available. This is most acutely observed in relation to zero-hour contracts, where daily, weekly or annual hours of work are not specified and the employee is required to be available, or not, by arrangement with the employer on a week-to-week basis (Cave, 1997a).

Workers are not paid to be 'on call' but only for the hours they work, and, although they theoretically have the right to refuse work, it is clear that both they and their employers generally regard the exercise of this right as an exceptional rather than routine option (Cave, 1997b; CAB, 1997). As no minimum working hours are specified, no minimum wage is guaranteed, although there are likely to be informal expectations on both sides which are generally adhered to.

In other contexts, however, flexible working practices linked to more standard contracts of employment may provide the employee with significant benefits; for example, where they are linked to family-friendly human resource policies. Part-time working arrangements, for example, can enable employees who otherwise would be unable to participate in the labour market to work in a way which fits with other responsibilities, primarily childcare (Watson and Fothergill, 1993). Both employers' (IPD, 1997) and employees' (TUC, 1998) representative organisations have commented on the positive potential for greater employment flexibility to enhance participation and productivity and there is some research evidence which suggests that flexi-time and arrangements allowing employees to work occasionally from home reduce absenteeism (The Industrial Society, 1997).

Defining flexibility: the evidence

Lack of reliable, comprehensive evidence about the structure and dynamics of contractual and working arrangements makes it difficult to monitor employment patterns and to assess the extent to which changes in employee resourcing and deployment indicate a significant change of direction in the way in which employment is organised.

- On one hand, there has been very little research which explores change in the balance of contractual relationships between employers and employees within specific contexts or which disaggregates trends in different sectors – but such evidence as there is suggests that aggregate change conceals wide diversity (Casey *et al.*, 1997; Robinson, 1999). Indeed, analysis of change in the sum total of, for example, temporary employment, may lead to underestimation of change throughout the economy as a whole, as shifts in practice in different sectors cancel each other out in employment statistics but, in practice, have substantial current and potential impacts on employment opportunities and working arrangements for particular groups of workers.
- In addition, a useful definition of what 'employment flexibility' encompasses is far from easy to construct. Terms such as 'non-standard employment', 'contingent employment', 'flexible employment', 'marginal labour', 'peripheral workforce' and 'insecure employment' are used by different analysts in different, overlapping ways and sometimes as if they were synonymous – when, in reality, each term covers a plethora of working arrangements, degrees of flexibility and objective levels of security or insecurity. Defining flexibility is exceedingly difficult. There is a permeability and

> fuzziness of boundaries: between occupational groups, within organisations, between organisations and geographically. In some cases, even the boundary of what constituted a job has disappeared or become irrelevant. Most research on the issues has either focused primarily upon numerical flexibility – and, within that, included different contractual relationships such as fixed-term, other temporary and part-time work, self-employed and inter-organisational sub-contracting – or on functional flexibility and flexible specialisation, mainly in manufacturing. More recent research is beginning to concentrate upon dis-aggregating separate trends and examining their relationship, in the workforce as a whole, in particular sectors and in specific organisations (Burchell *et al.*, 1999; Felstead and Jewson, 1999). This study is part of that trend.

The key is how employers deploy labour to match production or service demand. Available evidence suggests that employers have developed a range of methods to achieve this end, from establishing tenuous employment relationships with casual employees, to building in the requirement for greater flexibility – in terms of what they do and when they do it – from permanent, full-time employees. Such flexibility is observed, from a cost–benefit perspective, for employers and employees alike in order to understand the business contexts in which flexible contracts and working practices are deployed and the relative costs and benefits as they accrue to employers and employees respectively. If organisations facing similar product market pressures deploy significantly different human resource policies regarding working time, this would question the extent to which 'business pressures' provide an excuse for some of the more questionable personnel practices.

Thirty case studies were selected from five sectors to include a mix of examples where extensive use of flexible contracts and working arrangements was well-established, and where there had recently been increased use of such practices. In addition, the sectors were chosen to maximise the degree of variation between types of employment contract, type of work (skilled and unskilled work, high status and low status occupations), product market (business and consumer services, manufacturing) and type of organisation (size, structure, and ownership).

2 Flexible employment in Britain

Trends in flexible employment

Flexible labour resourcing covers a wide variety of employment contracts and working arrangements: temporary employment of varying contractual duration, part-time employment, fixed and variable shift-working, tele-working and other forms of home-working and indirect employment of various kinds – agency labour supply, labour-only self-employment and fixed-task consultancy. The core of this is the construction of jobs and determination of working arrangements by employers, which also incorporate job specifications and divisions of labour within organisations – and, also, determination of 'the effort–reward bargain'. Most recent UK debate on flexible resourcing and employment trends has engaged with the flexible firm model developed by Atkinson and his colleagues in the mid-1980s (Atkinson and Meager, 1986), where the authors discussed the ways in which employers appeared to be increasingly attempting to use numerical, functional and pay flexibility to maximise their labour force productivity. Numerical flexibility involves varying the numbers of staff employed over the working day, week or year to match labour demand as precisely as possible; functional flexibility requires employees to move among different tasks and operations as required, in order to maximise labour productivity; and pay flexibility attempts to tie earnings systematically to productivity or quality of performance – thus motivating staff to increase productivity and raise their performance levels. This, it was argued, reflected the increasingly competitive, unstable and segmented product and service markets of the late twentieth century, which required flexible specialisation rather than mass production and, as a corollary, new technologies and new ways of working (Piore and Sabel, 1984; Streeck, 1987; Wood, 1989).

It is certainly the case that the cumulative effect of industrial restructuring and economic recession throughout the 1970s and 1980s, nationally and globally, has been rising unemployment levels and polarisation between leaner, flatter, technologically sophisticated organisations – where the productivity of a 'downsized' core workforce is often supplemented by peripheral employees whose attachment to the labour market is relatively insecure – and sub-contracting enterprises whose survival in the market is contingent upon continued demand from larger organisations and is considerably more precarious. Although 'the collapse of work' predicted in the 1980s (for example, by Handy, 1984) has been less dramatic than projected by the most pessimistic analysts, the ratios of economic activity and dependency have shifted significantly. It has also been argued that there has been a transfer of risk from employer to employee and, by extension, to the State, as employers have progressively shaken out excess labour and adopted a 'lean organisation' model (Harrison, 1994). Current UK government policy is to encourage job creation, and reduce unemployment through facilitation of movement from welfare dependency into work, but a significant proportion of new jobs throughout the 1990s have been part-time or temporary employment (Cousins, 1999) and, for an increasing proportion of the workforce, job turnover rates have increased (Gregg *et al.*, 1997). However, the sharpest decline in full-time permanent employment occurred in the early 1980s, since when the decline has markedly decreased (Robinson, 1999). It is not yet clear, from analysis of labour market trends as a whole, whether recent growth in relatively insecure employment reflects a 'sea change' in human resource practices or cyclical response to economic pressures – but trends have clearly been different in different sectors and occupations and there has certainly been growth in perceptions of insecurity (Burchell *et al.*, 1999).

For those in employment, there has been an increasing probability that they will be in fixed-term or temporary employment and, for those without employment, that they will regain entry to the labour market via insecure, low-paid employment (Gregg and Wadsworth, 1996; Heather *et al.*, 1996; White and Forth, 1998). Analysis of Labour Force Survey (LFS) data reveals remarkable stability in the proportion of the workforce in temporary employment throughout the 1980s, whereas there has been a steady upward trend until 1997, particularly in fixed-term employment and temporary employees supplied by labour supply contractors (Beatson, 1995; Purcell, 1996). There is a growing body of evidence from particular firms of increasing use of contingent workers (Lester, 1995; Marsh, 1996; Rajan *et al.*, 1996) and from the temporary and contract staff industry of increasing demand for their services (Mintel, 1996; cf. FRES, 1998) but there has been little systematic analysis of how such labour resourcing practices are distributed across industry and occupational sectors. New patterns of management have clearly been emerging, particularly in terms of employer–employee contractual relationships, which deserve further analysis (Colling, 1995). How far do such patterns represent a general trend, particular practices within a range of sectors, or isolated and temporary responses to particular labour or product market contexts? And how far do they lead to enhancement or deterioration in employment opportunities?

The majority of UK employees in temporary work do not want a permanent job (Sly and Stillwell, 1997) – and so may provide a valuable and willing source of labour force flexibility for employers – although, like part-time workers, their lack of search for a permanent full-time post may reflect constraint rather than preference. Between the mid-1980s and 1997 there has been an increase in those reporting that they have taken both temporary and part-time jobs because they were unable to get a permanent or full-time one, from 9 to 12 per cent of part-time workers and 32 to 39 per cent of temporary workers (Robinson, 1999).

Changing contractual relations and attempts to match labour output and performance to demand have not been confined to those in 'non-standard' employment: as Harvey (1999) has pointed out, a common understanding of 'normal working hours' or a standard working week does not exist in Britain. 'Normal hours' vary among sectors and occupations and those engaged in full-time, permanent contracts of employment may be subject to a variety of flexible working practices relating to the deployment of their working time. The majority of employees in Britain, for instance, are subject to some variability in their working hours (Casey *et al.*, 1997). Within the context of the standard contract of employment, human resource policies have moved, in some instances, to providing a kind of two-way flexibility of benefit to employer and employee alike: for example, flexi-time arrangements where employees are contracted to work a fixed number of hours per day or week, but can vary the pattern of these, around a core or according to their preference, or work at home for part of the time.

The picture is complicated by the ways in which data have been collected and by confusion between different, sometimes overlapping, types of 'non-standard' contractual and working arrangements. Distinctions between outsourcing, in-sourcing, sub-contracting, use of fixed-term contracts between individual employers and employees or employers and self-employed consultants, use of directly employed temporary workers and use of employees supplied by the growing recruitment industry on an *ad hoc*, regular or labour supply contract, are sometimes not clear-cut and are impossible to monitor in national employment statistics. There is nevertheless clear evidence that the labour market has been becoming more risky (White, 1996) and that there is likely to be continuing polarisation between 'work rich' and 'work poor' households (Meadows, 1996). Although flexible work patterns (for example, fixed-term contracts and part-time employment) are increasingly found at all occupational and skill levels (Hewitt, 1996; Purcell, 1998), they have most often been characteristic of employment among disadvantaged groups in the past. This is no longer the case. The highest growth rates in temporary employment have been among professionals, managers and technically qualified employees, mainly on fixed-term contracts (Robinson, 1999).

One study of employers and employees carried out in six British local labour markets in the second half of the 1980s, which paid particular attention to the relationships between employers' labour force strategies and use of what the authors refer to as 'marginal labour' provided by the secondary labour force, and also considered the impact of contractual relationships on employee perceptions, reinforced this picture. It was found that employers' policies varied by industry group and by establishment size, but that, in practice, they:

> *... select from a very wide range of different policy mixes ... [that appeared to be] ... less the result of strategic choices designed to optimise the use of labour, than of piecemeal adjustments that reflected limited knowledge and the constraints imposed by the particular path of historical development of the organisation.*
> (White and Gallie, 1995: 261)

The same authors and their colleagues have subsequently concluded from a follow-up study conducted in 1992 that non-standard contractual arrangements had been increasingly adopted by employers at the start of the 1990s, but they continue to caution against grouping such workers together or making assumptions about relative job security and skill levels. Employees on non-standard contracts ranged in their study from insecure and disadvantaged through to highly skilled, self-determining employees in career entry posts.

This does not, however, contradict evidence from the mid-1990s of an increasingly strategic use of core–periphery strategies (Procter *et al.*, 1994; Purcell and Purcell, 1998) and, certainly, there is evidence of such human resource policies by major UK employers (Corfield Wright, 1996). The most recent employers' surveys specifically investigating employment flexibility have reported increases in the use of flexible workers and predict further increases (Institute of Management, 1996; Rajan, *et al.*, 1996; Casey *et al.*, 1997). Early findings from the 1998 Workplace Employee Relations Survey (Cully *et al.*, 1998) indicate increased sub-contracting, part-time employment, fixed-term contracts of employment and use of agency workers.

There has been concern that the most obviously one-sided flexible work patterns – exemplified by zero-hours contracts – disproportionately affect the most disadvantaged in society because of their concentration in low wage sectors of the economy (CAB, 1997). Moreover, the obvious disadvantages for insecure employees, particularly for those whose work patterns are erratic or pay and working hours are low, are amplified in the longer term by lack of entitlement to social welfare benefits (McKnight *et al.*, 1998; Purcell *et al.*, 1999).

It is questionable, however, whether forms of flexible work which disproportionately place the risk of the employment relationship onto the employee unequivocally benefit the employer. Recent research has drawn attention to the importance of 'the psychological contract' (Guest and Conway, 1997) and suggests, not surprisingly, that tenuous commitment from the employer tends to be mirrored by tenuous commitment from the employee, in terms of loyalty and performance. Research from the USA has demonstrated how minimum wage legislation – which inhibits the flexibility of wage levels – improved the performance of some low paid industries through encouraging employers to take a more developmental interest in their workforce. The provision of training and use of other sophisticated human resource policies were accompanied by increased performance and lower labour turnover rates (Kochan and Osterman, 1994).

Types of employment flexibility

As the following chapters will illustrate there was enormous diversity within the organisations covered in the study and in some cases the tendency was away from, rather than towards, flexibility and the increase of non-standard forms of work.

The key goal for our analysis was to evaluate how far different kinds of flexibility were used in tandem or as alternatives by employers. The key area of interest was the relationship between costs and benefits for employers and employees, but, in order to obtain some purchase on that, sense needed to be made of the diversity of working arrangements which were found in the sectors covered by the study. We attempted to 'map' the range of working arrangements which provide labour force flexibility to employers and indicate the provision, by employers, of 'non-standard' working arrangements which provide employees with opportunities to balance work and other responsibilities and objectives. An exploratory diagram has been developed which 'maps' types of arrangement according to the degree to which they are structured or unstructured, or permanent rather than temporary (see Figure 1).

There are problems with such a typology. In many cases, there is a strong subjective element in the determination of whether arrangements provide flexibility for either party: exemplified most vividly, perhaps, in agency temporary

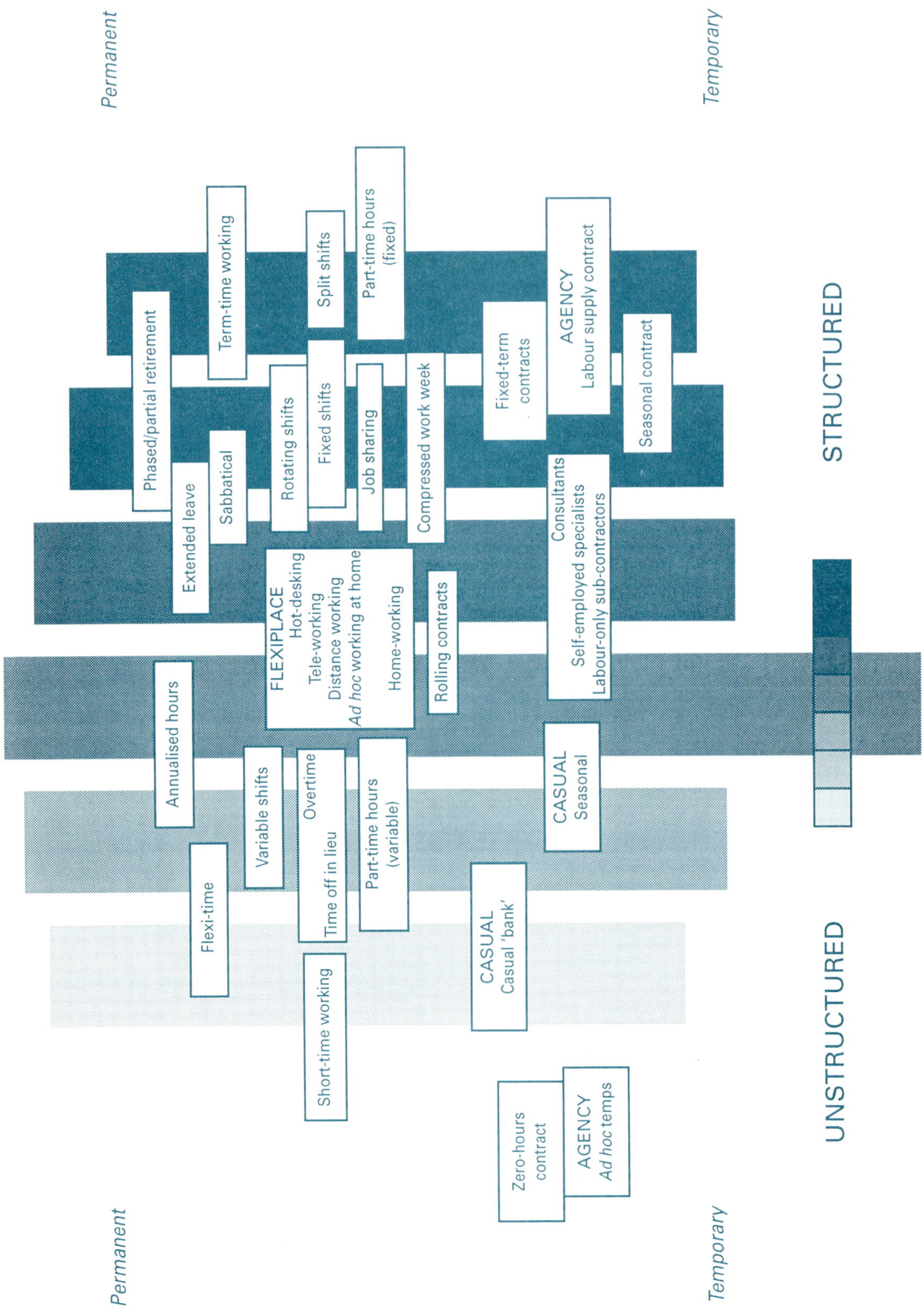

Figure 1 Typology of flexible working

placements. Agency work applicants whose skills are in demand may be able to pick and choose when and where they work – or, where their skills are less sought, may be able to obtain only erratic and unsatisfactory placements which do not meet their need for stable employment, a predictable level of income or, even, hours of work or a work location which is convenient for them. From the employers' point of view, such indirect employees may be regarded as a convenient source of labour supply which enables them to sub-contract personnel administration and tailor their workforce to meet their labour needs exactly on a day-to-day basis; or they may represent coerced dependency on an employment intermediary to supply transient employees with scarce skills at premium prices, when they would rather recruit permanent employees. Nevertheless, the diagram proved to be an extremely useful device in stimulating employers interviewed to talk about the issues and about the costs and benefits of different types of employment flexibility for them, and it has evolved as a result of these fieldwork discussions. The degree of structure involved in flexible working practices was found to determine, to a significant extent, the degree to which particular types of 'non-standard' arrangements were likely to be in the interests of the employer and the employee. Analysis of the findings was consequently undertaken using a somewhat less ambitious matrix which derived from the model, utilising the ranges of structured–unstructured working arrangements and temporary–permanent contractual arrangements.

Employment flexibility may be categorised by differing degrees of structure within particular working time or contractual arrangements. *Structured* flexibility is characterised by clearly defined boundaries of both working time and contractual status. Thus, for example, a continuous shift system with fixed hours of work is a highly structured way of organising working time; likewise a fixed-term contract places a finite boundary on the duration of that particular employment relationship. Conversely, *unstructured* flexibility refers to more loosely defined types of working arrangement or contractual status, where working hours are variable in terms of both time and duration or where the employment relationship is more tenuous. The structured and unstructured nature of differing arrangements is also cross-cut by the permanency of this employment relationship, giving rise to the fourfold classification on page 10 which derives from Figure 1.

Not all types of employment flexibility were found in all establishments, but all had a significant number of them and, in almost all cases, use of such 'non-standard' terms and conditions of employment had increased. As a general principle, most of those working arrangements in the top right hand corner of Figure 1 provide flexibility for the employer which has to be planned carefully – whether it is term-time working or provision of rights to take sabbatical leave. They may also have costs for employers – loss of continuity, short-term problems replacing absent staff – but they can be predicted and taken account of. From the employees' point of view, too, they may have predictable costs – but are also likely to have considerable benefits.

Conversely, in the bottom left-hand corner and, indeed, for most of the left-hand options, the impact for employers is virtually all positive, in terms of maximising labour flexibility and minimising labour costs. The disadvantages of such staffing would not be apparent in a situation of plentiful labour supply, but problems are likely to emerge in situations of labour or skills shortages, where recruits with wider options would be unlikely to choose such relatively insecure working arrangements. For such employees, the costs of temporary unstructured employment, both in the short term and the longer term, appear to outweigh by far the benefits, unless they have scarce skills and can both earn enough to be selective and choose where and when to work.

Examples of structured and unstructured flexibility

Structured, permanent: e.g. fixed part-time hours where those hours are organised to meet peaks and troughs in demand and cover a finite period at the same time each day and a constant number of hours per week.

Structured, temporary: e.g. a fixed-term contract with finite start and end dates, often related to a particular task or position where the permanent member of staff is absent for a fixed period such as maternity leave.

Unstructured permanent: e.g. annualised working hours where employees are allocated a fixed total of hours over the year and the exact distribution of these hours within this period is determined by different factors such as the volume of work or the non-work commitments of the employee.

Unstructured temporary: e.g. casual employment. In this case staff may work intermittently for the same employer for several years (as is the case in many hotels among casual workers), but ultimately the employer has no commitment to offer these staff any work nor has the employee any obligation to accept work that is offered. Thus the nature of the employment relationship remains highly tenuous and is limited only to the period of time for which the employee actually works. However, the introduction of the Working Hours Directive forces employers to recognise that they have wider responsibilities towards such employees – notably, the requirement to provide, *pro rata,* holiday pay related to the hours they have worked for the organisation.

Source: Institute for Employment Research

3 Approaching flexibility: a case study approach

Overall approach

The methodological approach was to carry out contextualised case studies and seek to collect data from employers, employees and other stakeholders concerned with particular organisations. From previous research findings, it was clear that sector and labour processes were key determinants of both past and current ways of workforce organisation and staffing, related to but not necessarily determined by product markets. The traditions of industries and the historically evolved structure of workforces have frequently been observed to influence the construction of jobs, for example, as full-time or part-time (Beechey and Perkins, 1986).

Thirty case studies in five sectors were undertaken. We were concerned to cover public and private sector employment and to gain some insight into differences and similarities between the ways in which small independent and large multi-divisional organisations accommodated fluctuation in demand for their products and services.

Choice of sectors, locations and case study establishments

The sectors selected were:

- financial services
- hotels and catering
- food manufacturing
- further education
- telecommunication services.

These industries allow for comparison across a wide range of employment conditions, all of which have been subject to considerable technological change and changes in both the external product markets in which they operate and in their internal industry organisational structures.

In addition to sectoral variables, an account of local labour market variables was achieved by choosing three contrasting localities. Within each sector, six establishment level case studies were undertaken, clustered in labour markets which exhibited different labour supply and demand characteristics. The areas chosen were Greater London, Tyneside (North East), and Greater Manchester (North West). Although all are essentially urban areas, they provided contrast in terms of having different labour market histories and structures. Unemployment was highest in the Tyneside area, lower in Greater Manchester and lowest in the Greater London Area (although it contained pockets of high unemployment). Strictly speaking, none of the areas included were limited to travel-to-work areas, either by official definitions or loosely understood, but they did constitute distinctive localities with particular labour market characteristics and contexts. In fact, there were no ways in which any of these localities stood out as having particular labour resourcing advantages or disadvantages, in general – although particular locations within the areas drawn upon, reflecting proximity (or not) of residential pools of labour, led employers to develop particular resourcing tactics, as will be discussed.

The case studies were establishment-based, although, in some cases, organisational boundaries were not drawn according to spatial establishment divisions and, indeed, sometimes varied according to function or administrative area, as will also be discussed.

Financial services

Banking and financial services have changed, particularly throughout the last decade, from a rather rigidly structured, oligopolistic professional services sector with distinct and regulated streams of expertise and well-defined opening hours, to an increasingly competitive market services industry where the range of products offered and type of organisation offering them have diversified. Information technology has radically affected the operations of the sector, the skills required of employees and the working arrangements in evidence. Twenty-four hour tele-banking, for example, has involved the setting up of information centres staffed round the clock, often by a range of flexibly employed indirect employees. An examination of recent Labour Force Survey (LFS) trends revealed that part-time employment is considerably lower in this sector than in the workforce generally, while self-employment has fallen dramatically since 1993, after the introduction of legislation designed to restrict entitlement to sell insurance to professionally qualified specialists. Temporary employment remains somewhat lower than average, but has grown more rapidly than in the workforce as a whole, particularly employment through agencies which almost doubled between 1995 and 1997.

Four finance organisations were investigated, enabling six case studies to be

Table 1 Finance case study establishments

Establishment	Area	Labour force*	Main operations	Type(s) of labour flexibility
Bigbank Central	GL	70 (61%)	Head Office Administrative section	Fixed-term contracts, part-time tele-working, 'hot-desking'
Norbank Centre	NE	1,500 (nearly 100%)	Banking (general)	Flexi-time, fixed-term contracts, part-time
Trendbank 1	NW	637 (83%)	Customer service call centre	Shift work, temporary staff, part-time, labour agency supply
Trendbank 2	NW	427 (95%)	Customer service call centre	Shift work, part-time, temporary staff, overtime
Westbank	All	46,600 (90%)	Banking (general): company-wide	Part-time, shifts, fixed-term, agency labour supply
Norbank Call	NE	– (150)	Customer service call centre	Shifts, fixed-term contracts

* Approximate percentage of current workforce on permanent contracts.

carried out, focusing at different levels of operation, as shown in Table 1.

In the case of Bigbank, we looked only at one central London head office administrative section, which allowed us to investigate the particular issues associated with the employment of specialist and clerical staff in the City of London. Norbank is a building society which has moved from mutual to stockholder ownership and broadened its range of services in line with finance industry trends. Two Norbank sites were included: the provincial Head Office and a customer service call centre. We included two Trendbank customer service call centres, which provide an interesting example of the increasing difficulty in defining boundaries within and among organisations. In terms of the services provided by the bank and much of the bank's personnel and administrative practices, these two sites operate as one 'virtual call centre'. Clients telephoning for service are automatically routed to one or the other according to staff availability; yet they are geographically distinct, in different labour markets, with different organisational histories, terms and conditions of employment and staff profiles. Trendbank 1 has been in operation for longer, staffed initially by existing bank staff from branches, supplemented by fixed-term, agency and 'auxiliary' workers as required. Trendbank 2 is a greenfield site with mainly new staff, recruited on the basis of 'people skills' rather than banking experience. They have mainly been recruited onto permanent contracts designed to accommodate the flexible working patterns required by the new, longer banking hours offered by the call centre, without incurring the traditional banking overtime rates. Finally, a case study of another High Street bank, looking at the organisation's UK operations as a whole, was undertaken at Westbank.

Hotels and catering

Hotels and catering has always relied extensively on seasonal and part-time employees, reflecting fluctuations in demand over the year, week and day for their services. The industry, however, has changed in recent decades from providing a relatively narrow range of accommodation and food service products to a highly segmented market where tourism, entertainment, business and leisure services (such as conference and fitness facilities) have transformed both the range of services offered and the skills required of employees. Employment has become considerably less subject to seasonal variation and, in fact, it is one of the few sectors where the proportion of temporary and fixed-term employees has declined in the 1990s (Purcell, 1996).

Part-time employment in hotels and catering is both considerably higher and rising more quickly than in general and, as an established area of female part-time concentration, is clearly one of the main areas of male part-time employment growth. Like the retail sector, it has increasingly drawn upon the student labour supply, particularly in fast-food outlets: recent research has revealed, at the extreme, that 60 per cent of the Pizza Hut chain workforce in 1998 were full-time students (IDS, 1999). Details of the hotel case studies are summarised in Table 2.

The hotels are thus disproportionately large employers, not representative of the sector as a whole, where over 80 per cent of businesses are small- to medium-sized enterprises (SMEs) with

Table 2 Hotels and catering case study establishments

Establishment	Area	Labour force[1]	Market segment	Main type(s) of flexibility used
Metroland Hotel	GL	74 (82%)	3* Business, leisure, local functions, small conferences	Shifts (inc. split), overtime, part-time
Grand City Hotel	GL	615 (80%)	5* Mainly international tourism and functions	Overtime shifts, casual and seasonal staff
Airport Hotel	NW	134 (83%)	4* Airline contracts, stopover, day conferences	Shifts, overtime, part-time staff
Provincial Posh Hotel	NW	408 (63%)	5* Business, non-resident leisure, conferences	Shifts, agency staff, regular casuals
Stateside North Hotel	NE	154 (88%)	4* Business, leisure, functions	Shifts, casual staff
North Chain Hotel	NE	118 (64%)	4* Mainly business and functions	Shifts, part-time and casual staff

1 Approximate percentage of current workforce on permanent contracts.
* Industry-wide star-rating of hotels, denoting quality of service and range of facilities offered.

an annual turnover of less than £250,000 per annum. However, focus on larger organisations can be justified on three grounds: first, there was significant acquisition and merger activity in the first half of the 1990s, resulting in a substantial increase in the industry share of larger employers and the proportion of the sector's employees; second, such organisations were deemed more likely to provide comprehensive insight into a range of 'non-standard' employment relations than smaller establishments; third, it has been established that they have considerable influence on industry policy and practice, including human resource management and employee development trends. The Metroland, the smallest of the hotels, is an established independently owned Outer London hotel; the Grand City, Airport and North Chain belong to British-owned multi-divisional groups; and the Provincial Posh and Stateside North are both part of American-owned chains – the former having been acquired by the multinational recently after a long history of ownership change and company mergers since its establishment as one of *the* luxury UK business travellers' hotels of the railway age, the latter a direct investment by another multinational designed primarily to serve evolving shopping tourism in the North East. The ratios of permanent to temporary staff in the hotels reflect largely the extent of non-resident business, its continuity and predictability. For example, the Grand City Hotel has renowned banqueting facilities which are used fairly continuously over the season from September through to June, whereas demand for the up-market provincial hotels' banqueting facilities is somewhat more erratic. Demand for functions catering, notably weddings, tends to cluster both in terms of days of the week and seasonally. Thus hotels where such activities are a substantial part of their business cannot provide continuous employment, but need to be able to draw on staff as required.

Food manufacturing

The food industry has changed in response to increasing consumer segmentation, catering technology, and food preservation and storage techniques such as cook-chill and irradiation. The industry has traditionally employed a substantial proportion of low skill disadvantaged workers. Technology has reduced the number of operatives required in many food factories and increased the demand for higher-skilled professionals and technicians, but a large number of low-skill jobs remain, and investment in technology has led to increased pressure to maximise its use by round-the-clock production and sophisticated shift patterns. As an industry where employment numbers have been declining due to increasingly capital-intensive processes, the ratio of temporary workers has increased in the 1990s, but has been volatile, indicating particularly high sensitivity to fluctuations in consumer demand and employer confidence. The food sector is one of the main areas of manufacturing where women are employed in substantial numbers and part-time employment is high by secondary sector standards, but it decreased slightly in the 1990s and represented only 15 per cent of the total industry workforce in 1997. Table 3 indicates the range of food manufacturing case study establishments.

The case study establishments within food manufacturing represent a diverse range in terms of ownership, product and employment. The smallest of the companies was independently owned and regionally based, whereas the others were all subsidiaries of larger companies, some of them multinationals, and operated in a national or international market. Those which operated predominantly within the domestic market tended to be heavily dependent on the demands of the large supermarket chains for business, which impacted upon the organisation for working time where products had a short shelf-life due to perishability or to particular promotional ties. All of the companies were engaged in continuous production. To a large extent the types of product determined the degree of technology and the level of skill required of each workforce. In the Frufood company, for instance, the majority of the work was undertaken manually and involved very little skill or technological know-how. In the other establishments there was more use of machinery and subsequently greater differentiation between grades of staff, with lower-skilled workers (often temporary staff) engaged in the most simple tasks such as packing. The level of female employment was generally low, although in certain establishments the management was attempting to attract greater numbers of women into the workforce by introducing more 'family-friendly' arrangements such as short part-time shifts.

Table 3 The food manufacturing case study establishments

Establishment	Area	Labour force*	Main products	Main type(s) of workforce flexibility
Bevfood	NW	430 (95%)	Packing and distribution of beverages	Annualised hours, shifts
Doughfood	NE	302 (90%)	Bread and cake production	Shifts, temporary staff
Icefood	GL	500 (90%)	Head Office of frozen food manufacturer	Family-friendly policies
Cakefood	NW	560 (75%)	Bakery products and ingredients, oils	Annualised hours, shifts, temporary staff
Frufood	NW	150 (70% – variable)	Prepared salads and soft fruits	Shifts, part-time staff
Spreadfood	GL	760 (95%)	Head Office of food and beverage manufacturer	Family-friendly policies

*Approximate percentage of current workforce on permanent contracts.

Several of the case study establishments had undergone a period of decline during the 1980s, resulting in widespread restructuring, and in some cases this had led to major job losses. This degree of volatility was still felt in some establishments and was reflected in the higher proportion of temporary staff employed there.

Further education

Further education has expanded in line with successive government attempts to develop a more streamlined approach to Lifetime Learning and the achievement of National Training and Education Targets (NTETs). Until 1992, further education (FE) colleges were funded regionally and terms and conditions of service were agreed by national negotiation between employers and trade unions, the details of which were published in what was known as 'the Silver Book'. One of the most controversial developments since the new funding regime was established has been deregulation of employment conditions in the sector, with a move to locally negotiated contracts and, in some cases, from collective to individual agreements between employers and employees. New contracts were widely introduced in the face of bitter opposition from the National Association of Teachers in Further and Higher Education (NATFHE) and there was considerable industrial relations conflict, which was still apparent in some of the case study institutions. In the academic year 1994–95 there were an estimated 1,500 redundancies.

Table 4 Further education case study establishments

Establishment	Area	Labour force*	Main FE provision	Establishment-specific increases in flexible patterns of work
CosmoColl	GL	843 (60%)	General FE	Fractional posts, part-time
OuterColl	GL	762 (57%)	General FE	Part-time, outsourcing, franchising
OutWestColl	NW	1,194 (40%)	6th form college plus adults	Direct temporary, outsourcing
CentreWestColl	NW	1,119 (36%)	General FE	Direct temporary, distance working, franchising
NorCityColl	NE	1,312 (33%)	General FE	Annual hours contracts, agency supply contracts, outsourcing
NorVocColl	NE	546 (40%)	General FE	Part-time working, outsourcing

* Approximate percentage of current workforce on either part-time or zero-hours, because permanent/part-time jobs not distinguishable.

Industrial relations deteriorated throughout the college system, but threats of further cuts and fears for their jobs defused much of the opposition from staff (Tebbutt and Marchington, 1997). Table 4 gives some indication of similarities and differences in the case study colleges.

Because some of the colleges had difficulty in discriminating between fixed-term, part-time and temporary staff, the proportions provided in brackets in column 3 are those on part-time, hourly or zero-hours contracts, which vary according to the subject-spread covered and proportion of work represented by sixth form provision. They were all general FE colleges with greater or lesser elements of vocational and sixth form education. These ranged from the smallest, NorVocColl, a former technical college with a strong engineering bias, to the largest, NorCityColl, an amalgamation of two colleges spread over four sites in geographically distinct locations. By far the largest proportion of part-time and temporary staff in all the colleges were teaching staff: the balance of part- and full-time depended on ratios of full- and part-time students, subject mix and college staffing strategy. All had and were continuing to widen their client base, develop new courses and cut unprofitable parts of their portfolios. For example, several had introduced distance learning programmes, were extending their hours of opening and were reducing the minimum number of students for whom a course could be deemed viable. All used virtually the full range of contractual and working arrangements covered by the investigation – for example, overtime working and part-time working – so that column 5 of the table indicates those areas of flexibility where there was said to have been recent or projected increase, which did vary somewhat among the colleges. All were increasing their use of functional flexibility, fixed-term contracts and variable-hours working, but some were also increasing part-time, direct temporary or agency-supplied employees and some were engaging in entrepreneurial activities such as franchising which involved the use of distance-working or home-based staff or sub-contractors. The key human resource issues were therefore restructuring, reorganisation and the new contracts. Redundancies remained a significant concern in several institutions and industrial relations were generally volatile.

Telecommunications

Telecommunication services is an industry which has gone through substantial change with the liberalisation of the telecoms market which saw British Telecom (BT)'s monopoly position eroded. The industry encompasses both relatively low-skill jobs (e.g. telephone chat lines) which typically offer non-standard forms of employment contract, and high-skill/high-pay jobs, such as those related to software and computer engineering, many of which are also attached to non-standard contracts of employment. Gender demarcations in established occupations have overridden technology in prescribing whether jobs were 'men's jobs' or 'women's jobs' and, even in high technology industries, gendered notions about 'appropriate' jobs for men and women, in terms of gender stereotypes, have proved powerful determinants of how jobs have been defined and constructed. Nevertheless, as employers have bought the 'flexible firm' concept, the organisation of working time and packaging of jobs have become more fluid as equal opportunities have become more accepted. LFS trends show a growing and volatile sector where women's part-time employment, although a relatively small proportion of the workforce, has more than doubled between 1992 and 1997, and self-employment has grown even more rapidly from a small base. The employment of temporary staff, particularly through agency placements, more than doubled between 1992 and 1997, which clearly reflects the burgeoning call centre industry – which is, of course, not restricted to telecommunications and illustrates the breaking down of boundaries between skills, sectors and jobs. The telecoms case study organisations are outlined in Table 5.

We were able to gain access to a range of organisations representing different aspects of employment in telecoms: BigTel, one of the largest multi-divisional communications providers employing the full range of skills and drawing on the services of every conceivable sub-contractor and employment intermediary; NewTec, a software design company employing mainly highly skilled specialists; ServTec, a somewhat larger and longer-established software and systems design partnership; WideTec, a cable installation company employing installation engineers and manual workers to lay cable on contract for the major ICT providers; and CallTec, providing information services – largely market-research for manufacturing and service industry clients, drawing on the ultimate 'flexible workforce' –

Table 5 Telecoms case study establishments

Establishment	Area	No. of employees*	Main type of business	Type of flexibility
BigTel	All	130,700 (% varies)	Telecommunications	Family-friendly policies
NewTec	GL	24 (87%)	Systems and software design	Annual hours, fixed-term contracts
ServTec	NW	104 (83%)	Systems and software design	Flexi-time/fixed-term contracts
WideTec	NW	291 100%	Cable installation company	Zero-hours, short-time working
CallTec	GL	3,000 (20%)	Information services provider, mainly operating call centres	Fixed-term contracts

*Approximate percentage of current workforce on permanent contracts.

mainly working on a succession of fixed-term contracts.

The analysis

Interviews were carried out with general and human resources managers at all the establishments and, in some cases, with additional management and administrative staff responsible for recruitment and staffing and with trade union representatives. In all but two of the establishments, employees' perceptions of the costs and benefits of non-standard contracts and patterns of employment were also obtained, either in face-to-face interviews, telephone interviews or by means of a self-completion questionnaire. In the chapter which follows, employers' use of non-standard employment in pursuit of labour force flexibility is discussed, followed by an analysis of their perceptions of its costs and benefits in Chapter 5 and the perceptions of employees in Chapter 6.

4 Employers' pursuit of employment flexibility

Introduction

Employers' human resource policies reflect choices made according to their perceptions of internal and external opportunities and constraints, as well as beliefs about the relationship between human resource management policies and organisational performance. Product market pressures, conditions in the local labour market, and the tradition of employment relations within the company determine, in varying proportions, the content of policies that are implemented. Increased competition may lead to employers attempting to minimise wage costs, or it might lead to the introduction of family-friendly policies to cut labour turnover, reduce recruitment costs and maximise return on training – it depends, crucially, on the type of staff employed as well as local labour supply.

This chapter is concerned, from the employer's perspective, with the introduction of working practices which sought a more flexible deployment of labour: particularly, more efficient use of working time. It is less concerned with functional flexibility, although, where functional flexibility was used as an alternative to numerical flexibility to take account of fluctuations in demand for production and services, it fell within the study's scope. The concept of 'the psychological contract' has become widely used to describe what the employee and employer expect from one another, beyond formal hours, task-fulfilment and payment, in the employment relationship (Guest and Conway, 1997). With reference to this terminology, a key question explored in this study is the extent to which flexible working time arrangements enhance or detract from the quality of the psychological contract between management and employee (Gallie, 1998). As the last chapter indicated, the establishments examined in different sectors were subject to similarities, both in terms of product and labour market circumstances and employment practices used to take account of these, so it is proposed to carry out a cross-sectoral analysis rather than examine the sectors separately – although specific sectoral aspects will be acknowledged where relevant.

Product market pressures

The product market pressures varied both between and within sectors. In the food manufacturing sector, for example, the challenge for the large employers was to maintain a continuous process that optimised the use of labour and technology to maintain price competitiveness in an international market. In the smaller establishments, the concern was with meeting the short-term demands of food retailers through a labour intensive production system. Mainly, product market demand was managed around a workforce that was full-time and permanent, with working shifts that had some variation around the usual hours worked: 51.2 per cent of employees in the industry have permanent contracts of employment coupled to variable hours of work (Casey *et al.*, 1997).

The food manufacturers mentioned three types of product market pressure:

- a need to satisfy short-term demand from food retailers

- the seasonal nature of production
- competition from other manufacturing sites (sometimes from within the same company).

In the most acute example, Frufood, which packaged prepared salads for food retailers, there was a labour intensive production system where employees were required to work ten hours of overtime a week at short notice. The product was highly perishable and retailers would increase or decrease their order, depending upon the weather forecast, at 24 hours' notice. Where seasonality was an issue, such as at Icefood, annualised hours had been introduced: for example, to deal with the short pea-picking season, employees worked much longer hours over the key summer period and less over winter. Though annualised hours removed the need for overtime with a concomitant impact on labour costs, it was not sufficient to provide competitive advantage in a sector or a company where annualised hours were commonplace; hence the need to customise annualised hours. For instance, Bevfood had established an additional hours system where employers agreed to work a limited number of extra hours over the year at no extra cost to the employee. This had been designed to safeguard the establishment's productivity against the parent company's other manufacturing sites.

It is apparent that in the food manufacturing sector where product demand was most uncertain, as in Icefood, that the company sought to manage this risk through highly flexible use of labour: staff had no option but to work the overtime demanded by management. A comparison can be made with CallTec, where

Case study: Bevfood

The key problem was how to cope with production peaks that accrued as a result of an increased workload, machine breakdowns, production failures elsewhere in the company. This had to be met without a substantial increase in personnel costs. The company's own preference was not to add to their headcount to meet what were, in effect, only intermittent production peaks. The solution had been a system that had some of the hallmarks of a 'call-out' wage premium. In return for a 4.5 per cent pay increase above a cost of living increase, workers agreed to work a potential 200 extra hours a year. The company paid for the 200 hours whether or not they were worked. Of these 200 hours, 120 would be 'Class A' that related to an increase in production, and 80 would be 'Class B' hours that related to production backlogs due to machine failure, etc. Although the flexibility agreement resulted in employees working an additional 79 hours a year, on average, the scheme had proved unpopular with employees because of its unpredictable call-out nature. Employees claimed that they were unsure when they would be required to work additional hours which they could not refuse to work.

The company's view was that it was paying for hours that were not worked and that it was deflating staff morale into the bargain. It therefore had decided to abolish the system through developing teams that took responsibility for their own production lines and managed their own deployment of time on the line.

Source: Institute for Employment Research

there was also highly uncertain demand for the company's product. Whereas the food manufacturer had attempted to meet demand through permanent contracts linked to mandatory overtime work, CallTec had managed the variable demand for hours through the use of zero-hour contracts, with largely part-time shifts. Arguably, the workforce was carrying a significant share of the product market risk faced by both companies, except that in Icefood, workers at least had the status of 'permanent employee' and the employment protection attached to that status.

Case Study: CallTec

The company employed 3,000 people, 80 per cent of whom were employed on zero-hour contracts as telephone operators in five call centres located in the UK. The company manned telephone centres on behalf of other companies. For example, if a company advertised its product and gave out a telephone line for enquiries, CallTec would provide that telephone service on behalf of the company.

At the site in the South East (550 staff), the largest in the UK group, telephone help-line employees were employed on rolling contracts which were related to the work available. If a marketing company wanted a telephone help-line number manned for three months, then employment contracts were offered for three months. In other instances, contracts only lasted for two to four weeks with staff levels fluctuating accordingly. One contract at the time of the case study visit lasted for 48 hours. As the company matured, it had been able to win longer-term contracts from companies, in one case for three years. The company provided all employees, including zero-hours employees, with 20 days' holiday (*pro rata*) and sick pay; otherwise statutory conditions of employment applied. On the other hand, a significant proportion of fixed-term contractees were students and second-job-holders who worked intermittently, and has been unlikely to stick around long enough to accrue holiday pay to any extent.

When the company was established in the UK, it took what contracts were available – mainly linked to sales campaigns – relying heavily upon students to staff telephone help-lines. Recently, several longer-term contracts, such as for a computer hardware company which ran for three years, had been won. This enabled the company to offer longer employment contracts; but the traditional labour supply often could not provide the continuity and commitment required to staff these.

The company operated a three-shift system – daytime/evening/night – plus weekend shifts. More callers were employed on the evening shift – up to twice as many as the day shift. Staffing was ultimately limited to the number of seats available. The company found that students were not committed to the work they offered, but they were flexible. The company could provide some continuous work where workers may be servicing a group of clients – the 'Response Team', for instance, handled responses to TV adverts for 30 different clients. Wages varied between £5 and £12 per hour depending upon the technical know-how required, whether the job was sales or service oriented, and whether languages were required. Staff, in the past, had not been viewed as a valuable entity. Now the company wants to get to a position where people can develop careers at the company – it wants people who are entrepreneurial in outlook and, in an increasing number of cases, have foreign language skills to work on several-country contracts. At the same time the company needs to recognise that good people are not interested in temporary contracts, as reported by the company's HR Consultant. To this end the company is developing different levels of telephone operator so that it can retain good people at higher levels. There was a high degree of turnover amongst staff, management reported, even though this was difficult to measure given the short duration of contracts.

Source: Institute for Employment Research

Hotels and catering is another sector where a variety of working time arrangements affecting manual staff have been introduced. Traditionally, hotels have solved the product market problem of fluctuations in demand over the working day by full-time employee shift-working and, particularly in food service and production, by split-shift working. Full-time employees, both shift-working operatives and craft-level staff, and (generally unpaid) overtime on the part of management and supervisory staff, provide one of the most flexible workforces of any sector.

The two five-star hotels, Grand City and Provincial Posh, had the lowest proportions of part-time employees in the sector, which reflected a considerably stronger adherence to traditional methods of working for high-income clients, reflecting a belief that their reputation rested on a particular style of quality provision. Thus, most jobs were constructed as full-time, apart from those which most obviously involved women's work – notably housekeeping, which was where most of the part-time employees worked in these two hotels. These were also the establishments that made the most sustained use of casual staff, mainly to service their banqueting and large function operations. Though all but the smallest establishment had 'regular casual' banks of effectively zero-hours staff on whom they could draw as required, the two five-star hotels' use of 'regular casuals' went beyond this, where they formed a significant and integral part of the full-time workforce – particularly in Grand City Hotel.

Case Study: Grand City Hotel

As an Inner London luxury hotel serving business and wealthy private clients, quality standards of service had to be maintained at a very high level, mostly achieved by the use of full-time 'professional' staff who had considerable experience of the industry. Because of its international reputation as a hotel – and also as an organisation prepared to train and invest in staff to ensure quality – ambitious chefs and waiters applied speculatively to work there, so the company in the past had done little advertising of vacancies. Informal recruitment prevailed – chefs introduced trainees from French hotel schools where they had contacts, for example, and waiters introduced their friends.

However, the banqueting business is seasonal, peaking in late autumn, Christmas and January and virtually negligible from July until September, and, apart from a 10 per cent core of permanent staff, was almost exclusively staffed by casual staff during the busy months. Around 90 per cent of banqueting staff were foreign. Food service waiters either 'passed through' for six months, or routinely worked for nine months. Some of the latter were regarded by the establishment as 'professional casuals' and there were between 15 and 20 who had worked for the establishment for 20 years. These workers were paid piecework, by the session, had no other fringe benefits, were not entitled to holiday pay or sick pay – although instances were cited of valued individuals being given sick pay. Ten per cent of casual banqueting staff were employed full-time, the remainder part-time; but of these 'part-time' staff, most worked part-time for other hotels. It was reported by the banqueting manager that most of them worked between 50 and 70 hours, for between 12 and 15 sessions.

At the peak of the high season, there were not enough silver service waiting staff and wine butlers to satisfy the demand from inner London hotels, and, although this particular hotel had less problems than many of its competitors, the banqueting manager had to work hard to ensure that his events were adequately staffed. Increasingly, specialist agencies were being used by both staff and employers.

Source: Institute for Employment Research

None of the hotel employers liked using agency staff because of the higher hourly costs, but, for Grand City Hotel even more than Provincial Posh, under-staffing would represent an unthinkable threat to quality. Where a high profile event required particular staffing, the Banqueting Manager would cross-subsidise staffing from other budgets to buy agency placements as required. The establishment had considered using 100 per cent agency staff but, the Banqueting Manager felt that the costs, in terms of staff loyalty and possibly service quality, would be too high.

Considered alongside Grand City Hotel, the example of BigTel in telecommunications, which sub-contracted an extensive range of operations and made significant use of agency labour supply contract staff in call centres, similarly provides a stark example of managing uncertain product market demand by externalising part of that risk to its workforce. Some of the larger establishments in the food manufacturing sector, hotels, and the banking industry instinctively rejected such an arrangement because, in their opinion, it denied the company the benefits that accrued from good employee relations – employee commitment, motivation, honesty, and so on – which ultimately impacted on worker productivity. The hotel and catering industry at the quality end of the market, though employing a number of 'professional casuals', was also against the over-casualisation of its workforce because of the impact this would have on the quality of the service it provided. Conversely, in some parts of the communications sector, casualisation – or, more typically, the use of fixed-term or zero-hours contracts – had been growing.

On the whole, the use of temporary staff in

hotels and catering is well-established, clearly related to product market fluctuations. The only recent change has been the increased participation of agency intermediaries in the employment relationship and, while this adds to employer costs, it may well serve to regulate the labour market and decrease employment insecurity for the workers involved. Companies such as CallTec capitalise on an interpersonally and sometimes linguistically skilled transient, young workforce. Their employment practices do not represent a deterioration of terms and conditions of employment, although they may reflect a net increase in the insecurity of available opportunities.

The further education sector, however, provides a further example where product market risk had been transferred to employees with the growth of casualisation and changing ratios of permanent and temporary posts within FE colleges. Whereas much of the numerical flexibility by use of contingent labour in BigTel, Icefood and Grand City Hotel involved primarily routine manual and clerical jobs, change in the further education sector has had most impact on professional teaching staff.

Since the creation in April 1993 of the Further Education Funding Council (FEFC) recently there has been significant structural change: close-downs, mergers and amalgamations of existing colleges and departments within them, accompanied by redundancies. Much of the change was cost-driven, partly to take account of reductions in the further education budget but also reflecting the government's approach to public services management over the 1990s. In 1993, the sector's 16 per cent increase in funding over three years required a 25 per cent expansion in student numbers which effectively constituted a budgetary reduction. In addition, demographic trends meant that the sector's traditional source of students – young people requiring vocational and sixth form educational provision – was dramatically lower in number than for several decades.

An illustration of how changes in the further education sector's market have affected employment relationships and the deployment of flexible working practices is provided by NorVocColl. Of all the colleges that participated in the study, NorVocColl had maintained the highest share of full-time staff, and as such is very much removed from what one might term a 'worst case example' of the impact of product market change on employment and the flexibilisation of work.

Case Study: NorVocColl

The college catered mainly for full-time vocational students. The Personnel Manager noted:

From 1993, incorporation, it was open trade. We were hit by a double whammy of competition from sixth forms and other local colleges and having to cater for 25 per cent growth at the same time.

Like all the colleges, the institution relied on 'permanent casuals' who were involved principally in teaching and learning support. Casual staff taught a range of hours per week, from three to 20 depending upon demand for their skills and their preferences. Casual appointments were made on an annual basis, with all casuals being made redundant at the end of each academic year in consultation with the relevant union and reappointed at the start of the next academic year. The college provided an Advisory Service for staff affected by this process, which in the first year was used by about 80 members of staff worried about their future employment, but three years later there were only three members of staff who asked for advice or information, reflecting what the management view as acceptance of the process. Casuals were administered by the college's own register, which was administered directly by the college.

The Personnel Manager went on to comment:

The complexities of employment law are enormous, and we are under a lot of pressure to use an agency instead, which would not have those set-up costs. But we feel strongly that the costs are outweighed by the benefits, in terms of the variety and expertise we are able to get from people.

Many of the casual staff worked in specialist fields such as radio journalism and, for such staff, teaching was a 'side activity' to their main job. It was noted by the Personnel Manager that some casual staff used the casual register as 'a foot in the door' while a minority pieced together hours working directly for the college and working at other colleges through an agency in order to create a full-time equivalent job.

Source: Institute for Employment Research

All the FE case studies revealed similar product market pressures to force increasing casualisation of work, but there were differences in the ways that these were managed, as will be discussed.

New flexibilities

The service sectors described above are, arguably, ones that have always needed to utilise employees at varying times of the day, where the Monday to Friday, nine-to-five contract was always inappropriate: further education colleges provide evening courses, hotels provide a 24-hour service, and telecommunication services is a new industry that caters for a 24-hour service demand. It is useful, therefore, to consider the position of a service industry that, until relatively recently, has historically deployed more regular hours of work. The banking industry has provided full-time permanent contracts of employment, a life-long employment relationship, and has operated with a well-developed internal labour market. Today, the life-long employment relationship appears to have been lost except for most senior management and the working time norm of nine to five, Monday to Friday, is now much less in evidence than hitherto. Linked to the change in the structure and type of work undertaken has been a proliferation of different types of employment contract: for example, fixed-term contracts linked to specific tasks, Tuesday to Saturday contracts, shift-work and so on.

Flexible employment in the sector varies by occupational position. For managers and more senior clerical staff, practices existed which sought to reconcile the family and working lives of individuals, or simply provide the individual with the autonomy to do their job to the best of their abilities (e.g. working from home when necessary). At the other end of the skill and status spectrum, work was more highly regimented – for instance, in call centres – and undertaken by employees with differing types of what may be termed non-standard contracts of employment (shift-work, fixed-term contracts, etc.). Flexible work patterns had developed for clerical staff engaged in the more traditional and established activities of the banking industry in branches, regional and head offices, that were of benefit to both employer and employee.

Staff in different segments of the banking industry faced different product market pressures. Many regional and head office staff were supplying internal markets to the bank that could be feasibly carried out over Monday to Friday, working 9 am to 5 pm. Branch staff too only needed to be on hand when the bank was open to customers over a limited range of hours. In the call centres and central administration centres there was a 24-hour operation over seven days a week and it was here that the more flexible types of employment relationship had been introduced. Trendbank 1 provides an example of how new types of contract were introduced with the establishment of call centres.

What is perhaps distinctive about the finance sector was the extent to which the industry was keen to develop other human resource strategies alongside the operation of flexible employment contracts which sought to secure a degree of motivation, satisfaction and progression for the employee – as will be examined in the case of Westbank in the next chapter.

Case Study: Trendbank 1

When Trendbank 1 moved over to a 24-hour a day operation at an existing call centre this necessitated the introduction of shift-working for existing banking staff. Previously staff had been contracted to work normal banking hours, so the move to shift-work necessitated substantial shift premiums to be paid. When a new greenfield site was opened, staffed wholly by new recruits including some long-term unemployed people, it was able to offer non-standard contracts which embodied flexible working hours without incurring shift-work pay premiums.

The bank has faced considerable pressure in its product market, as one of the smaller banks in its market. In many respects the company was one of the pioneers of 24-hour banking, but this position needed to be consolidated without a substantial increase in its cost base. Since call centres are fairly labour intensive, labour costs were a major area for cost containment. The older call centre had incurred substantial overtime costs that needed to be avoided at the greenfield site. This has been managed through offering employment contracts which required people to work non-standard hours without receiving higher rates of pay. The current priority of management was to negotiate harmonisation of contracts over the two sites.

Source: Institute for Employment Research

Labour market pressures

Outlining how employers organise labour solely with regard to the pressures of the product market suggests that they have considerable freedom in how they deploy their workforce. To a large extent, the introduction of flexible employment contracts is about obtaining a better match between product market demand and labour supply. Whilst one should not underestimate the amount of freedom some employers possess, such as CallTec, there are a number of constraints placed on employers when deciding about the organisation of their workforce. In the first instance, employers need access to employees willing to work the hours requested. As noted above, Frufood – a food manufacturer working at the lower end of the value-added market packing prepared salads and soft fruits – had severe employment retention problems relating to its use of overtime work. If a supermarket received a weather forecast of impending hot weather they would make a provisional order for a given number of units of packed salad and fruits. If the weather forecast changed over the next 24 hours the order might increase or decrease. The company insured itself against the risk of uncertain product demand by paying low wages – the lowest rate of £3.60 an hour recently increased from £3.10 – with a contractual stipulation that all employees might be expected to work an additional ten hours of overtime each week on top of the standard 40-hour week. It was apparent at the time of the study that the company had great difficulty in making the system work, even in a local labour market with a relatively high unemployment rate.

Case Study: Frufood

The establishment produced chilled foods: pre-packed salads, de-seeded melons, onions, pizzas, and so on to the food retail industry. The company had a turnover of £30m and employed 450 people. All orders taken from food retailers were provisional; on average orders varied by 20–30 per cent when made final, but they had been known to change by 70 per cent. The products that were processed had a short shelf-life, especially where they had been imported. This made it difficult to undertake adequate manpower planning, with the result that the company relied heavily upon employees working overtime at short notice and agency workers. Seasonal workers were taken on over the summer for two to three months on a full-time basis.

The company operated seven days a week using a fixed-shift system that relied upon full-time workers and a small number of part-time operatives – women on the 'mums' shift' which operated between 10 am and 3 pm. A three-shift system was in operation: 6–2, 2–10, 10–6. Labour turnover was high – over 100 per cent amongst line staff – due to the demand for overtime, usually made at the beginning of the new shift, and the low rate of pay (except on the 'mum's shift' where it was close to zero). Absenteeism was also reported as high, especially amongst the agency workers. The company paid £3.70 an hour for grade two staff (cutting melons) and £4.20 an hour for grade one staff (machine minding). A shift premium of £5 was paid for evening shifts, and £6 for weekend shifts. These shift premiums had recently been introduced in an effort to make the work more attractive. Overtime was paid at 1.5 times the hourly rate during the day, and twice the hourly rate after midnight and on bank holidays.

Unemployed people had been the main source of labour and this was reflected in the wage rates. The fixed-shift system was attractive to some people because it allowed them to take second jobs. The company relied heavily upon agency workers and without them the company could not meet the demand set by supermarkets. The more reliable agencies provided good quality staff, but the demand was sometimes so great that the company had to resort to 'less reputable agencies' with correspondingly 'less reliable' staff. On average, agency rates were £4.70 an hour, but the company had paid as high as £6.40 an hour. Agency workers were hired usually for eight weeks, but many failed to stay that long.

Source: Institute for Employment Research

The strong message to emerge from Frufood was that, where employers' and employees' needs coincided, as in the example of the 'mum's shift', then product market demand and labour supply could be successfully matched, but, where the workforce had a large part of the risk of an uncertain product market, they tended to exhibit low commitment.

The need for continuous use of production lines in the manufacturing sector requires employees to be on hand to operate the machinery. In some occupations, typically higher clerical, managerial and professional occupations, there is much less of a need to be in a specific place at a particular point in time. The Personnel Manager at Icefood, a head office of a large food manufacturer, characterised the work ethic of the establishment as one of 'presenteeism'. Management staff felt the need to work long hours because they thought that was what was expected of them, but, ultimately, it was reported, this was damaging to the company if only because it was believed that recruits of the highest quality would not be attracted to or retained by the firm. In response to this concern, the company encouraged clerical and managerial staff to leave at 3 pm on Fridays and managers were becoming increasingly open to the idea of staff varying their hours of work as necessary to accommodate their private lives so long as the business did not suffer. There was no established policy with regard to this type of flexibility – flexi-time operated outside of agreed hours, working from home, etc. – but it was left to department managers to set their own rules. At the higher end of the occupational hierarchy, establishments were developing the means to create flexibility at the margins of the organisation of work so as to ease the life of their clerical and managerial staff. This appeared to be part of a developing work culture which gave the employee a degree of autonomy regarding the organisation of their working day in return for which they would take responsibility for their workload and therefore would be willing to work late or additional hours when necessary. Elsewhere the application of such a system to manual workers was not nearly so apparent other than a few hours taken off in lieu, for example, to look after sick children when necessary.

Industrial relations and human resource policy

Several organisations sought to maintain and further develop a high-skill, high-wage, high-productivity workforce. In hotels and catering, concern with quality was largely reflected by a desire to minimise casual employment where possible and regularise it where inevitable. One of the most impressive hotel case studies was Airport Hotel, where the use of casuals has declined and there is a commitment, particularly by the Personnel Manager responsible for this hotel, to increase the proportion of permanent staff.

Case Study: Airport Hotel

It is regarded as an inescapable necessity for each department to nurture a 'bank' of potential casuals to accommodate fluctuations in demand. Students are positively sought, via catering departments in local universities and colleges, and are regarded as an excellent source of relatively 'high IQ' labour, who can often build their studies and social life around work opportunities and are thus very flexible, uninhibited by responsibilities to others. They are also seen as potential permanent recruits and three ex-casuals joined the company in the last year on completing their courses. The conference business here is less likely to be silver service than plated meals, so that training requirements are less onerous, but the proactive approach to recruitment was impressive. In the week preceding the case study interview, there were only seven casuals employed: three on catering for dinner for a two-night conference, four in housekeeping. These last four were students with 200-hour contracts, where the hotel has contracted to provide 200 hours of work and the employee to accept it, over an agreed period.

Source: Institute for Employment Research

It is a reflection of increasing competition for labour and concern with quality that employers in the hotel industry have become more concerned with minimising casualisation and have been seeking employment flexibility which meets the needs of employees as well as themselves. In the banking, food manufacturing, and further education sectors, trade unions have provided a restraint upon employers' ability to introduce non-standard and innovative working arrangements. In the first two sectors there were examples of the employers and unions agreeing to the introduction of flexible working arrangements, with the unions seeking compensation for employees where terms and conditions of employment were altered. At Bevfood and Cakefood, both highly unionised, the arrangements to alter the annualised hours and shift systems in operation were fully negotiated with union representatives. The extent to which the unions were able to resist or qualitatively alter the eventual outcomes of negotiation is difficult to gauge, but it did provide a barrier to management altering working conditions without regard to the views of the workforce. In Trendbank, initial union hostility to the revision of contracts to minimise overtime costs and facilitate increasingly flexible working has been succeeded by increasingly constructive partnership between the Banking, Insurance and Finance Union (BIFU) representatives and management locally and nationally.

The examples from the further education sector demonstrate the limits of union influence when an establishment is faced by severe competitive pressures in its product market, coupled to abundant supply of potential recruits, as the experience of CosmoColl illustrates.

Case Study: CosmoColl

The college was formed from the amalgamation of two colleges in 1992. Over recent years there has been a substantial amount of organisational change and a significant number of job losses: from 585 (full-time equivalents) in 1994/95 to 499 in 1997/98. The personnel manager reported that industrial relations were 'quite battered' by a wide programme of voluntary and a handful of compulsory redundancies that were liable to be extended further in the coming years. Two years ago the teaching staff contract was renegotiated to the detriment of staff in terms of the balance of teaching and other activities, fewer holidays, and the requirement to provide greater flexibility in order to cover the changed balance of provision: all-day Saturday operation, more higher education provision, adult provision, and community-based provision. In addition, there had been the elimination of all senior lecturer posts.

The key industrial relations issues were structure, staff profile, management levels and contracts. The college took a decision not to use agencies, for reasons of cost, but increased the use of part-timers where it was expedient to do so, referred to as 'fixed-term staff'. Approximately 300 staff were employed on fixed-term contracts. On the teaching side the contracts were for one year and for a variable number of hours, which could be zero. The college expected the balance in fixed-term to permanent staff to be increasingly in favour of the former over coming years. 'Most staffing decisions are entirely cost-driven', reported the Personnel Manager. Turnover was, nonetheless, low and further staff reductions will probably be required to accommodate cuts in funding.

Source: Institute for Employment Research

CosmoColl was by no means a worst case example. Elsewhere there has been a much greater willingness to take on agency workers in colleges to deliver teaching and with the underlying growth in agency and temporary staff the trade union's ability to gain influence in the workplace begins to evaporate, leading, indeed, to considerably worse union–employer relations.

As a public, unionised sector, FE has a tradition of strong commitment to equal opportunities and all the colleges had explicit family-friendly policies to a greater or lesser degree – a commitment to allowing for job shares, family-related leave and sensitivity to the need to accommodate domestic responsibilities. Formal commitment to family-friendly policies was also found in the financial and some of the telecoms and food establishments and, more informally, in hotels. It was where skills or labour were scarce that most effort had been made to meet employees' flexibility needs: for example, with respect to information technology (IT) staff, as in Icefood.

To a degree, IT staff occupy a labour market position that is characterised by one of surplus demand, but it would be mistaken to see the development of family-friendly policies simply as a response to labour market conditions. Though IT staff in particular appeared to possess the labour market power to extract a number of concessions from their employers – such as a key software engineer working entirely from home at NewTec – some employers recognised that such policies were of intrinsic benefit to the company. As will be explored in the next chapter, organisations such as Westbank recognised that family-friendly working arrangements were an important component of equal opportunities policy, and, although tight labour market conditions for some groups of employee certainly amplified the call for family-friendly arrangements, they were not the only cause of their introduction.

Case Study: Icefood

There was an acute problem with the recruitment and retention of IT staff in the London labour market. Accordingly, IT staff were allowed to work at home with the company providing the necessary technology (modem, PC, etc.) and the company was open to suggestions from the IT staff themselves about the type of working arrangements they required. Women returners had been identified as one particularly rich recruiting ground for IT staff and policies were being developed which would make the company an attractive proposition to such women. At the time of the study management reported that working from home or working variable hours was very much a new development that needed to be evaluated. Nevertheless, the company recognised that 'family-friendly policies' were required to recruit key IT staff and would prove beneficial if applied to other departments.

The company had used self-employed IT professionals to undertake special projects for them, but this had been limited to areas where the company had little expertise. Such arrangements would continue into the future, but for mainstream IT work the company preferred to use its own staff.

Source: Institute for Employment Research

Flexible deployment of working time

There are a variety of means that can be used to resource and deploy labour more efficiently, ranging from full-time permanent jobs that have a variable hours component to the casual employment of people as and when the work is available. The case studies capture this spectrum from examples where the employment relationship is strong, where one is looking at attempts to build some flexibility into permanent highly structured jobs (as with relatively high-skilled employees in further education, banking and food), to those where the employment relationship is weak, such as the use of zero-hour contracts, agency staff and casual workers (as in relatively low-skilled employment in hotels, and banking or telecom call centres). The business processes in all of the case study establishments and in all of the sectors necessitated flexible scheduling of labour in some manner. In its simplest case this has been concerned with obtaining variability around usual hours worked, such as the regulation of overtime; in other instances, it was concerned with more elaborate working time arrangements, such as split-shifts, annualised hours, etc.

Though each sector operated in distinct labour markets, management preference appeared to determine, at least as much as product and labour market pressures, establishments' human resourcing practices. Degree of constraint (for example, in the times at which goods and services have to be delivered) is clearly of crucial importance, but management solutions varied within as well as between sectors and there were common strategies and practices across the sectors. Agency workers, for example, are found in nearly every sector, as is the use of fixed-term contracts of employment, reflecting short-term and longer-term *ad hoc* or potentially unsustainable demand for labour – but the strategic choice of such contractual relations as preferred permanent mechanisms for the achievement of numerical flexibility was less apparent. Agency labour supply was used in the banking call centres as a temporary strategy in the face of change, and in food manufacturing, further education and hotels to meet labour shortages, which they would have preferred to meet with permanent staff or directly employed temps. Fixed-term contracts were used as 'test and try' recruitment in banking and further education, and also where future labour demand was uncertain; but were also used reluctantly in telecoms – particularly in software design – to enable employers to offer short-term 'no strings attached' inducements to attract scarce-skilled employees able to 'play the field'. Employers seeking flexible work patterns from permanent employees mainly used overtime, part-time working and shift-working throughout the sectors, but annual-hours contracts were used by particular employers in telecoms, food manufacture and hotels; spatial flexibility – tele-working and 'hot-desking' – was being seen as offering potentially mutually beneficial flexibility for employers and employees in banking – particularly in central London where office space is at a premium.

Conclusion

The chapter has demonstrated how flexible forms of employment contract are related to product and labour market characteristics and wider employee relations policies. A number of different approaches adopted by employers have been identified:

- the increasing transfer of risk attached to the product market to the employee, as witnessed in the further education sector and some call centres in the banking and telecommunications industry
- the pursuit of greater flexibility within permanent employment contracts
- an equal opportunities commitment to family-friendly policies that encapsulate a more variable deployment of working time
- an *ad hoc* response to product and labour market pressures as and when they arise.

The returns obtained by employers from their approach to creating a flexible workforce are addressed in the next chapter.

5 Costs and benefits: employers' perspectives

Introduction

What are the costs and benefits faced by employers deploying employment contracts containing varying degrees of working time flexibility? It appears that, from the employer's perspective, flexible working time agreements were largely motivated to achieve the following benefits:

- the ability to match production demand with labour supply, especially the need to meet peaks in demand
- reduction in labour costs from better matching of labour input and production demand (e.g. lower overtime costs)
- flexibility to meet periodic crises in production or service provision.

The costs accrue where the employment relationship results in:

- higher labour turnover
- increased absenteeism
- poor labour relations
- increased personnel costs (e.g. from higher recruitment costs).

The extent to which benefits outweigh costs depends upon the skill with which workforce flexibility is designed and managed by employers. The evidence presented below suggests that the most tenuous forms of employment relationship between employee and employer amongst, for example, routine grades of manual and non-manual worker, can impose significant costs on the employer with higher absenteeism and labour turnover feeding through to lower productivity. Piecemeal attempts to introduce flexibility into standard employment practices may be as significant as non-standard practices, both in achieving workforce flexibility and changing employer–employee relations.

Flexibility within the full-time permanent contract of employment

In the food manufacturing sector, containing overtime pay was a severe resource allocation problem. The examples of Bevfood and Cakefood demonstrated how two large manufacturing sites devised schemes to meet periodic peaks in production without paying overtime to their manual workers or hiring additional workers (below a certain critical level of production). The majority of staff at the two establishments were permanent full-time employees – although both had a substantial complement of employees on fixed-term contracts whose terms and conditions were otherwise the same as those of permanent staff. Both were highly unionised, and both employed a system of annualised hours that incorporated a variable element so that additional hours could be worked to meet unforeseen production demands. The annualised hours system at both establishments was comprised of a basic set of hours to be worked in each year (basically 36 hours a week over 47 weeks) plus additional hours to meet peaks in production and take account of production backlogs and machine failures. Management could call upon the additional hours to be worked at 24 hours' notice.

Bevfood and Cakefood historically had been staffed by full-time permanently employed production workers and both establishments anticipated that this was how they would be staffed in future. The benefit of such an approach to staffing was the degree of loyalty and motivation they obtained from employees and this was deemed central, by management, to the establishments meeting the performance goals set by the parent companies. Low labour turnover and increased productivity meant few projected vacancies for permanent jobs, with fixed-term appointments used to cover for, amongst other things, long-term sick leave and work on special projects. Both establishments paid relatively high wages for their localities and had no difficulties recruiting the labour they required. This may be compared with Frufood, which operated with a lower profit margin on its goods, much shorter lead times, and lower skill mix.

Frufood, as illustrated in the previous chapter, relied upon permanent staff and also required overtime to be worked at short notice. Here there was little consultation with the workforce regarding the operation of the shift system and no union was recognised. Bevfood and Cakefood were confident that, once the working time arrangements were working satisfactorily, a 10 per cent saving in labour costs could be obtained. At Frufood, the inability to devise a system that signalled overtime work led to both high labour turnover and high agency worker costs. Demand for Frufood's products (ready prepared salads) was highly elastic and the goods had a short shelf-life. It attempted to insure against this risk by paying relatively low wages (just above the legal minimum) for low-skilled work with a contractual stipulation that employees should work ten hours of overtime each week on demand. The costs this imposed on the company were high: high labour turnover (over 100 per cent in some departments), poor staff morale, and high costs attached to the use of agency workers. The Human Resource Manager reported that she needed to maintain a flexible deployment of working time through mandatory overtime (subject to legal limits). The balance between the costs this imposed on the permanent workforce, leading to high quit rates, and the cost of agency workers required to meet peaks in demand and cover for the high quit rate, was an optimum one given the company's trading position. The balance between increasing the wage rate to retain staff and thereby reducing agency wage costs required fine judgements to be made. The level of increase in wage rates across the board necessary to retain staff was thought, for the time being, to be in excess of the costs of hiring a small though substantial number of agency workers. The situation, however, was under constant review. The company thought that the low level of skill required by production line jobs was such that there was little scope to implement policies to improve job satisfaction and suchlike in an attempt to improve productivity rates and lower the quit rate. The productivity rate, it was reported by management, was established within reasonable limits by setting the pace of the packing machines. A comparison of the costs and benefits incurred by Bevfood and Frufood is provided in Table 6.

Table 6 Employers' costs and benefits of flexible employment relationships: manual production workers

	Bevfood (mainly annualised hours)	Frufood (mainly overtime + temps)
Costs	Industrial relations problems when production demands cannot be met through existing agreements Additional hours paid for but not necessarily used Relatively high wage costs	High absenteeism/labour turnover High agency costs Risk of not meeting orders Lack of attention to work by staff (especially agency workers)
Benefits	Overtime abolished Production demands met through existing working time arrangements Workforce commitment to working time arrangements Devolving of production line responsibilities made possible Low labour turnover/ absenteeism	Reduced labour costs – when system works Numerical flexibility

Source: Institute for Employment Research.

Two-way flexibility within the permanent employment relationship

Within the permanent employment relationship employers' concerns relating to the flexibility of manual workers centred around constraining labour costs, especially overtime payments. In industries such as banking that employed large numbers of non-manual workers, often in moderately skilled jobs attracting wages similar to those of skilled production workers, labour cost containment was also an issue – hence the large number of redundancies over recent years in banking – but concerns over overtime pay were much less in evidence. This resulted from the flattening of the organisational structure and growth of more individualised appraisal and employee development relationships, hence the emergence of a two-way flexibility between employer and employee that has developed, to a large degree, separately from the wage effort bargain. This is perhaps more common in an office environment within the banking sector rather than the more regimented call-centre environment.

By two-way flexibility is meant the degree of reciprocity whereby the employee will be readily allowed a few hours off work for whatever reason, say to take a sick child to the doctor, in return for which they may stay behind one night at work to finish whatever task needs completing. The nature of the arrangement may well be tacit. The employees know that they will be allowed time off should they need to take their child to the doctor; managers know that they can rely upon their staff to work late should it be required. With respect to the permanent employment of clerical workers the emphasis was very much upon creating a working environment that allowed a degree of *ad hoc* variability around usual working hours (usually around the core hours stipulated in flexi-time arrangements), either at the behest of the employee or the employer. Given that many permanent clerical workers in the case study establishments were women, it was felt that this was making a contribution to family-friendly practices where women had a primary care role for their young children. It was very much an informal system that was encouraged by central human resources function but left to line managers as to whether or not they wanted the system to operate in a given manner. The benefits of the arrangement were that the employer could call for additional hours to be worked without having to negotiate overtime payments, and an environment was created where people were not clock watching.

Alongside the development of two-way flexibility, and central to its operation, was a wider set of human resource policies that supported it. Two-way flexibility recognises that both employers and employees have needs that potentially conflict with one another unless a framework is put in place that attempts to reconcile the potential conflicts. Westbank was concerned to strike the right balance between family and working life.

Case Study: Westbank

The company expected to reduce its staff by over 5,000 people over the coming five years. This placed a considerable pressure on the business to maintain employee morale and avoid, wherever possible, compulsory redundancies. To this end, the company was attempting to find ways of redeploying people across the bank in an effort to retain knowledge within the company and avoid the costs of redundancy.

Even though the company needed to reduce the number of its employees over the coming years there was recognition of the general need to retain people and recruit new people into the company. Driven in part by the company's commitment to equal opportunities and a desire to retain experienced staff with family responsibilities, the company was in the process of implementing the Developing Work Programme. The aims of this programme were as follows:

- To achieve a better balance between home and work lives, in part through easing working from home.
- To develop more flexible procedures to retain people who might otherwise leave the company.
- To enhance the company's record on women in senior management posts.
- To achieve more benchmarking with external organisations.
- To introduce more flexible employment contracts in the branches so that the business is better served.

Overall, the Developing Work Programme was

forecast to save the company £400m in recruitment costs and productivity savings by the Year 2000.

Source: Institute for Employment Research

The Westbank Developing Work Programme applied to both routine grades of non-manual staff and professional and managerial employees, but its potential application was not specific to the banking sector. Food manufacturing and telecommunications services also reported the development of policies which attempted to build a degree of flexibility into the jobs filled by managerial and professional staff. In most instances, companies were more content for policies to be designed and promoted by the human resource functions than to allow individual departments to establish their own practices. There was, however, a consensus across many firms that management and professional staff needed to have some flexibility built into their working lives so that the accommodation of work and family was more sensibly balanced.

Table 7 outlines some of the costs and benefits recognised by employers relating to the variety of flexible working practices in operation with respect to permanent non-manual and professional and managerial workers.

For industries such as banking the development of two-way flexibility was based around a high degree of trust between employer

Table 7 Costs and benefits of flexible working arrangements for those on permanent employment contracts: non-manual and professional and managerial staff

	Routine non-manual staff	Professional and managerial staff
Costs	Low numerical flexibility Occasional inconvenience/ staffing difficulties Lack of continuity (e.g. in job-share)	Can lead to static workforce, lack of 'new blood' where no growth
Benefits	Development of an *ad hoc* flexible employment practice Equal opportunities strengthened Abolition of overtime Healthy 'psychological contract'/ loyalty Reduction in turnover/cuts 'natural wastage'/reduces replacement and training costs	Helps attract and retain diverse, committed managers Health and safety benefits where long hours' culture is broken down Healthy 'psychological contract'/ loyalty Reduction in turnover Retains and enriches experienced staff

Source: Institute for Employment Research.

and employee and supported by a wider set of human resource policies, but this was often being developed against a background of staff reductions, which invariably introduced a degree of tension into the employment relationship. Against a background of possible or probable redundancies the balance between the degree of flexibility offered to and expected from the employee can be lost, where employees compete to demonstrate commitment to the organisation.

Fixed-term employment contracts

The majority of managerial and professional workers were employed as permanent employees except in a few instances: IT staff who were much in demand were occasionally hired on a self-employed basis, for example at NewTec, Norbank Centre, and Spreadfood. Two head offices, however, reported that they were keen to develop more project-based work that would require specialist managerial or professional skills. In the past when the establishments had hired specialists an expectation had been developed that career development would follow on from their appointment. In practice this had been exceedingly difficult to deliver and the companies felt that they had been mistaken to raise, even inadvertently, staff expectations of career progression. In future, such staff would be recruited on fixed-term contracts for the duration of a particular project. In several instances, establishments had struggled to find professional IT staff. Often IT staff preferred a temporary engagement with the company or to work on a self-employed basis on a particular project. Because of embargoes on new teaching appointments at some of the FE colleges, allied to approval of building in an unproblematically probationary period, most recent FE professional appointments had been on fixed-term contracts. This had led to difficulties in making appointments in some cases. Where specialisms were scare, good applicants could not be attracted to relocate for one- or two-year contracts with no guarantee of continued employment.

Unlike professional and managerial staff a substantial number of clerical staff were employed on fixed-term contracts or other forms of temporary contract. For the employer, the benefit of using flexible employment contracts was the numerical flexibility they afforded. Staff on temporary or fixed-term contracts, sometimes linked to non-standard hours of employment, provided the means to fill temporary increases in demand without adding to the headcount in the organisation. For many organisations, especially in the banking sector, the headcount was a sensitive issue. Temporary labour tended not to be included in the official count of employees – an important consideration for some managers – and such staff were ineligible for the non-wage rewards provided to permanent staff. Though the value of non-wage rewards in the banking sector has been reduced over recent years they are often still generous by comparison with other sectors.

By hiring new recruits on fixed-term contracts the company provides itself with an extended probationary period for the new member of staff which acts as a prolonged screening device. Even where a contract was terminated and the company was unable to continue employment, that person joined a group of individuals to whom the company will turn to first should a permanent or another fixed-term employment become available, thus providing a pool of potential staff not unlike the hotel banqueting staff identified: although consisting of younger candidates, most of them sought more stable employment. The banking sector over recent years has had a number of special projects, such as the conversion of building societies into banks, that have required a short-term demand for clerical staff. Norbank, for instance, was reluctant to engage permanent full-time staff for jobs that would then become redundant once its conversion from building society to bank had been completed.

Case Study: NorBank

The company was involved in converting its status from building society to bank. This necessitated the establishment of a call centre that would answer the questions of existing account holders. The employment this created would cease as soon as the conversion process was completed and customers' enquiries tailed off. The call centres needed to be staffed by individuals who had the necessary social skills and intelligence to deal with sometimes complicated and sensitive issues. The company through its recruitment policies was able to obtain the employees of the calibre it required and though, in most instances, it was unable to continue their employment once the conversion was complete, it had developed a recruitment pool to which it would turn first when vacancies emerged. Given the qualities the bank had requested of its fixed-term appointees, this was considered to be a particularly rich pool of staff the company wanted to take advantage of in the near future. In fact the company had been able to make use of this recruitment pool for a number of permanent vacancies that had subsequently arisen.

Source: Institute for Employment Research

Production workers too were subject to fixed-term contracts. Bevfood, Doughfood, and Cakefood all hired employees on fixed-term contracts. The rationale in all cases was to meet temporary peaks in demand for whatever reason: such as production backlogs, launch of new products, cover for sickness, etc. Like Norbank and Trendbank, the use of fixed-term contract employees provided the employer with a pool from which it could recruit permanent employees if a permanent vacancy arose at a later date. Management expressed some doubts about the loyalty and commitment of staff on fixed-term contracts – would they, for example, recognise and stop a malfunctioning machine as quickly as a permanent member of staff? – but in all three establishments the fixed-term contract production workers had been employed for several years on a continuous succession of fixed-term contracts or had been employed on several occasions as fixed-term employees. At Bevfood the Personnel Manager reported that there was uncertainty about the number of people who would be employed at the establishment over the medium term. One means of protecting the numbers employed was to fill each new job with a fixed-term employee, but he was reluctant to do this because of the benefits that stemmed from having permanently employed staff. The costs and benefits of fixed-term contracts as they accrue to the employer are outlined in Table 8.

Table 8 Costs and benefits of fixed-term contracts

	Non-manual workers/ manual workers	Professional/managerial staff
Costs	Sometimes low levels of work commitment Lack of company loyalty from temporary employees	Higher rates of pay for certain groups (e.g. IT specialists) Doubts about company loyalty Failure to attract strong candidates
Benefits	Numerical flexibility Cover for absent workers Avoids use of agency workers Recruitment pool established Allows for trial period	Allows staffing of special projects Allows experts to be brought in on *ad hoc* basis No need for development of specialist careers No commitment to employment continuity beyond period required

Source: Institute for Employment Research.

Agency work

Several establishments in the food manufacturing sector, hotels and catering, banking and finance, and further education relied upon agency workers to meet production or service needs. The main criticism of using such workers was the expense of doing so – at Frufood, described above, the hourly cost of agency workers could be twice that of permanently employed production workers. Cakefood also noted that the habit of using agency workers could create its own dependency upon them: where an establishment has always hired agency workers to meet production peaks there was a tendency to use this as a management tool of first rather than last resort when planning production schedules.

Though employers were critical of their use of agency workers on the production line, and critical of the quality of staff often provided by agencies for low-skilled work, where agency staff were employed in office environments there was often a more favourable response on the quality of worker provided. This may well relate to the different rationales of individuals with differing skills applying to agencies for work, which is discussed more fully in the next chapter. The costs and benefits to the employer of using agency workers are outlined in Table 9.

Zero-hour contracts

The extent to which a zero-hour contract actually constitutes a contract between employer and employee is questionable. If the employer only agrees to pay the employee when work is available it is not obvious when the contract actually comes to an end and the employee is eligible to whatever entitlements they are due. The employer could state, in perpetuity, that no work was available. Thus the

Table 9 Costs and benefits of hiring agency workers

	Production workers	Non-manual workers
Costs	Labour available when required Labour supply and administration handled by agency	Can fill in at short notice Generally good standard of employee from agencies Labour supply and administration handled by agency External perspective can be refreshing
Benefits	Performance unpredictability of agency workers Creates dependency within company High absenteeism Lack of commitment/low effort Higher hourly cost of agency workers	Relatively high expense of hiring agency workers Lack of commitment/low effort Lack of continuity/insider knowledge

Source: Institute for Employment Research.

contract is never terminated but no work is made available either.

The benefit to companies of providing staff with zero-hour contracts was that labour supply was matched almost perfectly to labour demand. Demand to some extent could be predicted because the number of peak calls was related to an event such as a television or press advertisement where a contact telephone number was announced. The evidence from CallTec suggests that the almost casual nature of the employment relationship between employer and employee could suit both sides, since the employees (students, mothers, etc.) often had other principal interests around which they could fit their paid work. However, as the company attempted to become involved in higher value added services it found that the labour supply it had targeted was not ideally suited to its new needs. To this end the employment relationship was under review.

The costs and benefits of using zero-hour contracts are shown in Table 10.

Retreat from the casualisation of work

The food manufacturing and banking sectors relied mainly upon permanent and fixed-term contracts to meet their labour needs. Hotels and catering, telecommunications, and further education relied much more heavily upon contractual relations that are designed to supply labour only when it is needed, such as hiring casuals, agency workers, or employees on zero-hour contracts. The extent to which this is a response to the highly specific market

Table 10 Costs and benefits of using zero-hour contracts

	Production workers	Non-manual workers
Costs	No commitment to be available as required May result in high turnover of staff requiring greater predictability	No commitment to be available as required
Benefits	Enables labour costs to be tightly controlled and fit demand Flexibility provided by regular staff with inside knowledge Ability to adjust staffing at very short notice No commitment to provide regular employment or particular working hours Can provide mutually negotiable flexibility on a day-to-day basis (e.g. family-friendly) resulting in high commitment and satisfaction	Staff only there (and paid) as required Flexibility provided by regular staff with inside knowledge Ability to adjust staffing at very short notice No commitment to provide regular employment or particular working hours Can provide mutually negotiable flexibility on a day-to-day basis (e.g. family-friendly) resulting in high commitment and satisfaction

Source: Institute for Employment Research.

conditions they face, an issue of labour supply, or a combination of other factors, varies according to particular circumstances. What is apparent is a desire of some companies to move away from the highly flexible deployment of labour where this is thought to affect adversely quality of service. Hence in the hotel and catering sector, which has a tradition of hiring casual staff, there is evidence that some companies are trying their best to move away from the casualisation of work. Similarly, the telecommunications call centre was reviewing its use of zero-hour contracts as it attempted to move up the value added ladder. In contrast, the further education sector appeared to be largely moving in the other direction, increasing employment insecurity.

Within the hotel industry there is a requirement inherent in the services provided, to a greater or lesser extent, to match employment patterns to fluctuations in demand for labour. In general, the industry has a reputation for low-wage, low-skill employment, low investment in training and development, poor human resource management and high staff turnover. There have, however, always been pockets of relatively good practice and recent evidence suggests that increased competition may be generating more widespread attempts to move beyond management rhetoric that it is a 'people industry' to more pragmatic concern for effective employee resourcing and development. This was observed in several of the hotel case studies. Non-standard employment patterns – part-time working, shift-working, casuals, and fixed-term contracts – have been commonly used by the industry to accommodate peaks and troughs in demand for services over the day, week and year.

The use of highly flexible employment contracts in the hotel and catering sector can be obtained from the example of the Metroland Hotel, which had attempted to provide a structured working environment where staff were employed on permanent contracts even though they may have to work variable or split shifts. Agency workers were generally only recruited where staff – typically chefs – were in short supply. The desire of all the case study hotels to provide a high class of service and to be gauged on their customer care capacity, from the smallest to multinationals, led to nurturing of employment relationships, even where employees had been employed on a regular casual basis for many years, as in the banqueting suite at Grand City Hotel.

Case study: Metroland Hotel

As the smallest establishment included from this sector, the hotel approaches the requirement for flexibility over the working day and week by a balance of full- and part-time permanent staff, with a strong emphasis on team-working, multi-skilling, variable hours rotas, and overtime working. As a Greater London establishment, the company was particularly susceptible to competition for staff, especially scarce skilled categories such as chefs. It has had to recruit increasingly further afield and advertise across the country, in the national trade press, as well as recruiting locally and through agencies. It pays above-average rates: the lowest-paid employees earn £4.25 per hour and hourly-paid staff are paid time and a half for overtime. Salaried staff work 'as and when required' and can take time off in lieu. Agency staff were only used when it was impossible to appoint directly, being seen as costly and less likely to become fully integrated into the team ethos; but recruitment difficulties were indicated by the fact that there was one chef and two kitchen porters recruited through an agency at the time of the case study fieldwork.

High employee commitment is sought, in return for good conditions of employment, willingness to train and develop staff and willingness to respond flexibly to employees' needs. For example, in food and beverages, hours are arranged for a working mother to fit in with her husband's ability to care for the children. Outsourcing has been considered for the restaurant, given the extremely competitive environment in which it operates, but it was decided instead to invest in current staff skills to raise quality and facilitate innovation. For example, the current Head Chef has been with the hotel for 17 years and has been encouraged to research the competition by eating out once a week at his employer's expense and report back with ideas about menu and presentation. With their contract of employment, employees are issued with a document outlining management philosophy, which emphasises commitment to the customer and quality service, team-working and management's commitment to training and developing staff.

Source: Institute for Employment Research

The costs attached to shortages of people with particular experience or skills led to upward pressure on wage rates. This could be offset by the use of agency workers, which few of the case studies had been able to resist, but which added an element of uncertainty to management of those functions where they were employed. On the other hand, all the hotels employed students, either directly or via agencies and, in the case of both the Airport and North Chain hotels, they had taken strategic decisions to source this highly competent, flexible and willing pool of labour whose own need for flexible work opportunities could be matched with their own requirement for unsocial hours working.

The example of the hotel industry may be compared with the further education sector where a much more volatile employment relationship had developed between employer and employees. Here much less emphasis had been placed on avoiding the casualisation of work – although again, where the required flexible work opportunities of self-employed specialists such as designers who wish to combine practitioner and teaching careers can meet the colleges' need for hourly-paid teaching staff, the two flexibilities can be of mutual benefit. There are more staff with 'atypical' patterns of employment in FE than in most sectors. At best, these are contented portfolio workers; at worst they are multiple-job-balancing, under-employed and insecure workers having to balance spatially and substantively varied workloads for several employers to make a living income. It is not always clear how far employees will be able to ensure that they build up appropriate National Insurance and holiday pay entitlements as a result of such 'jobs-juggling', despite their rights under the Working Time Directive.

Conclusion

The evidence reveals that unstructured flexibility may suit a business working at the lower end of the value-added spectrum (in some hotel and telecom establishments), or requiring relatively low-skilled workers of whom there is a convenient and reliable supply (such as in some hotels), or with unpredictable requirements for contingent workers to supplement a core of more stable employees (as in FE, food production or banking). To the extent that quality control is important for organisations, or they require employees with skills in short supply, or fluctuations in demand for their products or services are predictable, they require structured flexibility. In short, employers wishing to manage human resources effectively need to maximise the quality and reliability of their employees and it appears that they are more likely to feel able to do this with permanent, highly motivated workers: those with whom the psychological contract is of mutual trust and willingness to accommodate two-way flexibility. This was the case with both highly skilled software designers and IT specialists in NewTec, Icefood and ServTec, and with low-skill workers such as the 'mums' shift' in FruFood and room attendants in Airport Hotel.

6 Costs and benefits: employees' perspectives

Introduction

This chapter focuses upon the employee perspective on flexible working arrangements and non-standard forms of contract. What are the costs and benefits for employees of different ways of working and how effectively do they permit staff to reconcile work and non-work commitments? The costs and benefits of flexibility – and the lack of it – are assessed in relation to the structured or unstructured nature of the employment relationship and related working arrangements. The flexibility of these impacts upon employees' lives in different ways according to the socio-economic characteristics of workers and the labour markets in which they operate.

A diverse range of working arrangements and contractual relationships was found among the different occupational groups at each case study establishment, as indicated in the preceding chapter. The key issue is which flexible working arrangements are of benefit, and to whom? Evidence from the case study establishments presented in the remainder of this chapter seeks to address this question by outlining the flexible employment strategies pursued by or forced upon employees in tandem with the costs and benefits which accompanied them for different groups of workers. The analysis revolves around two major areas which play a key role in employee satisfaction and commitment: the organisation of working time and the security or otherwise of contractual status.

Working nine to five? Clerical workers and flexible working time

The majority of clerical staff included in the sectors studied were found in financial establishments, as call centre customer service operators and processing clerks within bank head offices. As the majority of these clerical workers were women, many of them with family commitments, their key concern was how far they could reconcile work with their family responsibilities.

In the Trendbank financial call centre, tightly regulated working hours were organised to meet fluctuations in demand over a continuous 24-hour shift system. Staff were offered a variety of shifts and were able to specify which rotation they preferred to work. A number of these were part-time shifts encompassing the hours of 9 am to 1 pm or 10 am to 2 pm, while various full-time shifts stretched across the entire 24-hour period. Many staff were able to find a pattern of hours which suited them.

- Some women welcomed the opportunity to combine office-based work of regular hours with their family responsibilities. Serena, in her mid-twenties with two young children aged four and six, found that working the morning shift was convenient for her because she could start work after they went to school and finish in time to be at home when they got back.
- Mike, a student, found that working a few shifts per week during the evening allowed him to supplement his income during term-time, and he was able to work full-time at the centre during holidays.

The major issue faced by employees was how to cope with change, particularly in the more established site where the majority of workers had been accustomed to a traditional nine-to-five day. When people needed time off at short notice, or when their circumstances changed and they could no longer continue their initial shift pattern, they could encounter problems. If staff wanted to switch rotation, they could only do so by 'bargaining' with their time so that the needs of the call centre were not compromised. From the employer's point of view this was a satisfactory arrangement because it enabled them to staff more unpopular shifts at the weekends and in the evenings, by in effect 'penalising' those staff who wanted to change. Enforced trade-offs were often involved if staff wanted to alter their shift pattern.

Judy, a part-time customer service operator in her early fifties, wanted to change from a key evening shift to an already over-manned daytime rotation. To do so she would have to work every other weekend as well, as her employer sought to bolster call handling capacity at this increasingly busy time. She was reluctant to sacrifice her weekends but felt increasingly that she would be forced to do so.

Although the call centre was a highly structured and in some respects inflexible environment, staff there exhibited a high degree of satisfaction with their ability to combine work and family commitments. Being able to choose from the menu of different shift patterns available certainly allowed women like Serena to access office-based employment that suited their domestic arrangements, for example. The highly structured nature of working hours meant that all staff worked fixed shifts and overtime was rare: this gave staff predictability, making it easier to plan ahead and organise their own time. However, it also meant that unpredictable demands on staff time, such as needing time off to look after a sick child, were often difficult to negotiate over the longer term. Being tied to the call centre and its shifts meant that there was no autonomy over working hours, such as being able to leave work half an hour early and make up for it by working over lunch. Hours were fixed and ultimately geared towards meeting the needs of the business, and this resulted in lower levels of satisfaction with the availability of time off when required and managers' understanding of the competing demands on staff time, as Table 11 shows.

Table 11 Satisfaction with working time at the Trendbank call centres

'Family-friendly' working arrangements?	Employees (%)
I can combine work and family life	79
Management is understanding about my family commitments	59
Time off is always provided if I need it	64

Source: Institute for Employment Research – 'Whose Flexibility?' employee survey.

Workloads had increased markedly in recent years at Norbank, due to growing consumer demand and the pressures arising from internal restructuring, resulting in the progressive extension of extra hours working. Although this establishment ostensibly offered a standard nine-to-five working day, this increasing number of extra hours was perceived by many staff to be encroaching into personal time.

Over two-thirds of staff surveyed at this banking headquarters worked extra hours, many of them working more than five hours overtime per week. Although clerical and junior management staff received a premium rate for overtime, the majority of those working extra hours did so reluctantly, either because they perceived it to be expected of them – 'required as part of the job' – or felt it was necessary to get all of their work done. Even though staff enjoyed some autonomy in organising their hours, via a flexi-time scheme, many of the benefits of this appear to have been eroded by the informal spread of overtime working.

Table 12 shows that a significant minority of staff working here expressed disaffection with their ability to manage work and family life and the main area of contention appeared to be among full-time staff who felt that the opportunity to reduce their hours by eliminating overtime or switching to part-time work was limited.

Table 12 Satisfaction with working hours in Norbank

Working hours?	Employees (%)
Satisfied with hours	55
Prefer less hours	36
Prefer more hours	0
Prefer different hours	9

Source: Institute for Employment Research – 'Whose Flexibility?' employee survey.

This case illustrates the problems which can arise for staff when working time is treated as an elastic property. The clerical staff at Trendbank 2 perceived few benefits to be gained from working extra hours, other than the extra income, and for many (principally those with family commitments) the advantages of this were outweighed by the infringement of work into non-work time.

Where staff had more influence over their hours, there appeared to be higher levels of satisfaction with the organisation of working time and in particular the balance between work and home life. Flexi-time and annualised hours systems were highly effective in allowing staff to achieve a 'workable' balance between their home and their job, where the autonomy they offered to staff was not eroded by excessive overtime. For example, flexi-time and job share schemes for clerical and support staff were operated successfully in several FE colleges and telecoms companies. In many of the factory offices, staff perceived such arrangements to be helpful in allowing them to meet their family commitments, as well as a sign that they were entrusted by employers to regulate their own hours, differentiating them from the majority of production workers in these establishments.

Helen, a 50 year old part-time admin assistant at an FE college, had benefited from the job share scheme at her workplace which allowed her to combine work with raising her family:

I job share and work Monday, Tuesday and half of Wednesday. I work 15 hours because children can be hard work and this is just enough for me. By Wednesday afternoon I'm finished work and have time for my family.

Clerical workers and contractual status: the growth of 'permanent' temps?

In several cases, staff who were contractually employed on a non-permanent basis had in fact been employed as temps for several years by the same company. This caused a degree of frustration among some employees of which management was often aware. Several organisations were consequently engaged in a process of shifting long-standing casual employees onto a more structured contractual relationship (typically by offering them a fixed-term contract). However, in some cases, the offer of a fixed-term contract rather than prolonged 'casual' status may result in the erosion of employment rights which have accrued over time.

In Trendbank 2, a number of long-serving casual customer service operatives were being transferred onto three-month renewable contracts in an attempt to reduce turnover and enhance job security. However, this left some of the staff wondering why they had not simply been taken on as permanent, as they continued in practice to be 'permanent temps'.

Joanne, a 22 year old worker at Trendbank 2, had been moved to a temporary contract after working as a casual customer service operator for over a year. Since then she had been employed on a series of three-month contracts and was frustrated with the ongoing lack of security offered by her job:

I was employed as an auxiliary full-time for 17 months before being given a temporary contract. I am now on my third temporary contract. It's hard to feel content in a job if it isn't secure.

Temporary employment at an establishment was often perceived as an effective 'way in' to more secure employment there. Certainly in cases where there had been sustained expansion of the business, such as the initiation of a new service like a call centre, this was found to be the case.

The costs and benefits of different kinds of flexible working practices and contractual relationships for employees working in clerical and secretarial positions are outlined in Table 13.

Flexible working hours for management and professional staff: fighting a long hours' culture?

For those in higher level occupations, the willingness to work overtime was often taken for granted and went unrewarded in financial terms. The benefits for such staff of working extra hours were perceived in terms of career development. Putting in extra hours was seen to be a part of the job by the majority of management staff across all the establishments we visited. Workloads were high, and many managerial staff in particular felt that working overtime was a necessity rather than a matter of choice: over two-fifths (44 per cent) worked extra hours primarily so that they could get all of their work done. This raises important issues in terms of both psychological well-being and equal opportunities at work (Kodz *et al.*, 1998; Mills, 1999).

Table 13 The costs and benefits of different flexible working practices and contractual arrangements for clerical/secretarial workers

Type of flexibility	Benefits	Costs
Permanent structured	**All sectors** *Flexi-time*: degree of autonomy to organise workload and manage working hours to suit family commitments *Part-time working*: ability to combine work and family commitments **Finance** *Fixed shifts*: regular and predictable working hours	**Finance** *Fixed shifts*: some unsociable working hours and difficulty getting time off
Permanent unstructured	**Finance** *Long working hours*: overtime premiums	**Finance** *Long working hours/overtime*: infringement of work into non-work time
Temporary structured	**All sectors** *Fixed-term contracts*: an opportunity to access permanent employment within the organisation	**All sectors** *Fixed-term contracts*: lack of job security
Temporary unstructured	**Finance** *Casual work*: scope to combine office-based employment with studying	**Finance** *Casual work*: lack of job security, insecurity of earnings and irregular hours

Source: Institute for Employment Research – 'Whose Flexibility?' employee survey.

Within the two telecoms sector companies that employed mainly specialist software personnel, the situation was somewhat different. Highly flexible annualised hour and flexi-time schemes were in operation which devolved much of the responsibility for organising their working hours to staff themselves, most of them highly qualified professionals. Because work at the software companies was largely project-based, staff could vary their hours within an annualised framework to fulfil work commitments and achieve a satisfactory balance between work and non-work time. Frequently the existence of such provision became a key attraction for prospective recruits, particularly those with family responsibilities.

Table 14 Working hours among managerial and professional staff

Working hours?	Employees (%)
Satisfied with hours	43
Prefer less hours	46
Prefer more hours	5
Prefer different hours	6

Source: Institute for Employment Research – 'Whose Flexibility?' employee survey.

In NewTec, a small independent software company comprising predominantly degree-qualified analyst-programmers, all staff – full- and part-time – were able to work flexible hours. The company provided outsourced IT services to a large financial establishment and so work volumes could be controlled and a three- to six-month planning frame had been implemented which provided ample notice of increased demands (such as installing a new software system). The flexibility afforded to staff resulted in high levels of employee commitment. The company was found to be a particularly attractive employer among highly qualified female software personnel, who found that the combination of flexi-time and the conciliatory attitude of the management towards family-friendly policies (such as provision for staff to work part-time after maternity leave, and allowing part-timers to organise when they would work to suit their family responsibilities) was a key element in their decision to join the company.

Table 14 illustrates attitudes to working hours among managerial and professional staff.

Sarah, a programmer in her late thirties with young school-age children, had been working part-time at the company for a year since being made redundant from a previous job elsewhere. From three job offers she chose this particular company because it had the 'people-friendly' attitude she was looking for, allowing her to manage successfully her time between work and family commitments.

Casualisation and professional staff

Among professional staff, fixed-term contracts were predominantly found in the telecoms and FE sectors, with contrasting results which reflected the buoyancy of one sector and the heavy cost pressures and organisational restructuring within the other. In the case of highly qualified and experienced software engineers in the telecoms companies and at some of the financial organisations, being on a temporary contract was viewed largely as a status symbol which brought with it lucrative financial rewards.

Contractors at telecoms NewTec were paid double the salaries of permanent staff and were generally employed to add specific skills and knowledge to a project, for three- or six-month contracts. The benefits to contractors – apart from the lucrative financial rewards – were that they could take their pick of projects and control their own workloads. On the downside, they were responsible for their own training (in non-work time) and received none of the employee benefits, including profit-share scheme, enjoyed by permanent staff.

> 'You can't blame them for taking the money, but it's not all a bed of roses', said one of the company's permanent employees. 'A lot of them move around and don't build up the same working relationships as you would find with other staff. It can be quite an isolated existence.'

In ServTec, managers disliked having to use contractors, not only because of the cost premiums involved but also because of the resentment that this sometimes caused among existing staff.

> 'Some of them do come in and shoot their mouths off about how much they are earning', said one manager. 'It does antagonise the rest of the staff sometimes. A couple have left to become contractors themselves and they were probably unsettled by the contractors we've had working here to an extent. There's a lot of demand around at the moment because of the Year 2000 problem and they know that they'll always be able to get a permanent job if they want. One has already left to go contracting for a couple of years and has recently been re-employed permanently again.'

In contrast, college lecturing staff employed on short-term contracts often felt aggrieved with the situation and the uncertainty which arose from it, affecting both their professional and personal lives. The greatest disaffection was expressed by lecturers who had already established themselves in the profession and were attempting to build a career. Many who responded felt that temporary contracts, particularly if they were on a part-time basis, made it more difficult to motivate themselves to engage in additional activities such as organising courses and the administration required of the more senior level positions they were aiming towards. They felt a lack of attachment to their work and their colleagues, which was felt to inhibit the likelihood of career progression.

CosmoColl offers a good example of the pressures faced by staff within the FE sector. Since incorporation the college had made radical staffing cuts to reduce costs and was employing more staff on fixed-term and hourly-paid, casual contracts because of unpredictable demand for teaching in some subjects. Contracts are issued on 31 August in theory, but actual teaching schedules for the term ahead may not be confirmed until October or November, depending on demand for courses – resulting in high levels of anxiety and insecurity among contract staff.

It was regarded as increasingly difficult to take on course leadership on hourly-paid or fractional posts because of higher administrative loads associated with new forms of course management and assessment.

> Anne, a part time lecturer in her mid-thirties employed on a fixed-term contract, found it difficult to invest the extra hours in her job because she was uncertain about her contract renewal from year to year. She felt that as a tutor she was not performing as well as she could because she felt lacking in control of her own work. She also felt uncertain about her

job, even though her contract had been renewed several times in the past.

Job insecurity contributes to low morale and lack of cohesion in staff teams. I don't feel part of the team and I never know what my hours will be from one term to the next.

It is clear from interviews with temporary lecturers that the insecurity they experienced led to low morale and it is likely that teaching quality may have been threatened (Husbands, 1998). In those colleges with high proportions of hourly-paid and term-time contracts, low morale among all teaching staff was a big problem. Institutional policies such as employing all new staff on temporary contracts eroded the confidence of everyone – permanent as well as temporary – in their own job security, by sending out the message that resources were tight and demand uncertain (Gallie and White, 1995). For some, of course, short-term contracts and hourly-paid positions were a choice rather than a constraint: these tended to be younger staff seeking an entry into the profession, older staff on the verge of retirement, or specialists who took the opportunity to supplement their main income through teaching. The overall effect of casualisation had been to erode staff confidence and morale, however, and some of the colleges were recognising this by gradually moving their hourly-paid staff with long-standing service records onto less precarious fixed-term contracts where teaching hours were more stable. Table 15 illustrates the costs and benefits of different working arrangements for professional and managerial staff.

Working shifts: operatives in food manufacturing, hotels, and telecoms

Shift-working was a common feature for operatives within food manufacturing and the hotel industry, and the organisation of working time in these establishments provides a useful comparison. Shift-working has always been traditional in both industries and is invariably seen as 'part of the job' by employees. However, in hotels, the prevalence of variable shifts and in particular part-time shifts 'slotted in' to the working day at peak times meant that there was greater scope to control the number of hours staff worked from week to week. Ironically, coping with unpredictability was a greater issue for those working more structured shifts than those working at such variable times.

In the food manufacturing sites, shifts operated in a three- or five-crew pattern to cover 24-hour production schedules. Most staff did not consider working shifts to be a problem, although the majority here were full-time men who had often been working in the factories for several years. Where overtime was available, the inconvenience of working extra shifts was mediated by wage premiums, and changing to a five-crew pattern was offset by having several days off in succession.

Joe, a 52 year old production worker, was ambivalent regarding the five-crew shift pattern he had been working for several months:

The five-crew is okay as you get more days off in-between, so you can do things like some work around the house or go away for a couple of days. What we don't like is being mucked about from shift to shift.

Table 15 The costs and benefits of different flexible working practices and contractual arrangements for managerial and professional workers

Type of flexibility	Benefits	Costs
Permanent structured	**All sectors** *Fixed shifts*: ability to plan ahead predictably and (sometimes) to set particular working hours to suit needs *Part-time hours*: ability to work to fit in with other commitments	**Food, finance, hotels** *Rotating shifts*: physically and socially disruptive **All sectors** *Part-time hours*: (often) inability to earn living wage **Hotels** *Part-time hours*: (often) unsocial hours (e.g. breakfast service)
Permanent unstructured	**Telecoms and FE sectors** *Flexi-time/annualised hours*: degree of autonomy to organise workload and manage working hours to match volume of work	**All sectors** *Long working hours*: difficult balance between home and work
Temporary structured	**Telecoms sector (and some telecoms personnel within other sectors)** *Fixed-term contracts*: high wage premiums **Telecoms and FE sectors** *Fixed-term contracts*: scope to control work assignments, ability to move in and out of the labour force	**FE sector** *Fixed-term contracts*: low morale and security, impact on career development **Telecoms sector** *Fixed-term contracts*: low attachment to colleagues, responsibility for own training and development
Temporary unstructured	**FE sector** *Zero-hours/casual contracts*: ability to move in and out of the labour market and decide when or whether to work	**FE sector** *Zero-hours/casual contracts*: uncertainty of working hours and income, limited scope for career progression

Source: Institute for Employment Research.

However, the system of annualised hours outlined in Chapter 5 was disliked by staff in Bevfood, who felt that they were being called on to work extra hours with little consultation and with no visible reward.

The presence of a number of women working as full-time operatives at the factory heightened the issue of overtime, as being asked to work an extra couple of hours at the end of a shift was problematic if childcare arrangements had to be made or family commitments met. Staff felt that they had little input into the process of mobilising extra hours and resented the last-minute demands that were occasionally made of them, however infrequently.

Carole, a mother in her late twenties, commented:

Once they asked me to work another two hours at the end of my shift ... I tried to get out of it but I couldn't. My little girl was left crying in the school yard as I wasn't there to pick her up on time.

Source: Institute for Employment Research

The new system restored some of this control by devolving responsibility for organising overtime to staff teams who could more accurately identify when overtime was required and organise who would do it. Staff had more confidence in the 'fairness' of the new system. By giving them greater control in organising extra hours, management was able to strengthen the attachment between team members, relying on informal bargaining between staff to achieve a 'win:win' situation, where management obtained the flexibility required and staff were prepared to give up some of their non-scheduled time in return for the hours back at a later date. One potential aspect of this system which staff were concerned about was that those who had been trained on more than one of the machines might be disproportionately called upon to work extra hours because of their functional flexibility.

Bevfood is an interesting example of how the presence of more women in the workforce led to a less formally structured arrangement of working hours where overtime was concerned. Management could no longer rely on the willingness of staff to work extra hours in return for higher premiums when they were already working full-time shifts, as family commitments took priority in the rest of their time.

Several of the food manufacturing sites were experimenting with the idea of introducing part-time shifts into the production schedule, specifically aimed at attracting more female employees into the workforce. Invariably these part-time shifts were geared towards production requirements, but it was felt that they would also offer more family-friendly employment to local women, largely with few qualifications, who might not otherwise be able to access employment.

This echoes practices which have been occurring with the hotel sector for several years. Here part-time employees comprise over two-thirds of the workforce (Hospitality Training Foundation, 1996) and part-time shifts are scheduled into the overall shift system to cover periods of high demand. While full-time staff at all levels tend to work long and highly structured hours, part-timers are often afforded more flexibility as they are looked upon as a valuable resource to provide cover at busy periods or if others are off sick such as at North Chain Hotel.

Part-timers (generally women in low or unskilled jobs) were able to specify how many hours they wanted to work at North Chain Hotel.

One woman was employed initially to work 26 hours per week. After six months she decided that she would like to reduce her hours to 18 so that she could have more time for herself, but two months later she returned to the Personnel Officer requesting that her hours be increased again to 22. With fewer hours she had missed the companionship of work and found that she had too much spare time on her hands.

The degree of flexibility afforded to staff at the hotel was of course mediated by the need to ensure adequate staffing levels, but because there was a long-standing register of casuals – mostly students who were constantly pressing for work – management was in a position where it could allow part-time staff to experiment with different working hours until they found something that was right for them. In this case, the employer had made a positive choice to meet the needs of valued part-time staff in order to minimise turnover and allow for the hotel's extensive in-company training policies to take root.

In several of the hotels, it was common practice to ring round staff to come in at short notice or to ask staff to stay on at the end of their shift to cover a particularly busy period. Working extra hours was seen as a valuable 'top-up' to the weekly earnings, but not wanting to let down colleagues was also an important motivating factor, with strong bonds forged between staff working alongside each other, where perhaps greater satisfaction was gained from the social interaction of work than from the work itself. This is an established finding among employees in relatively low-skilled work, where social relationships are often found to be the most satisfying aspect of the job.

Among technician-level staff in WideTec, project-based work sometimes shifted the responsibility to work long and unsociable hours onto employees rather than allowing them freedom to choose when to work. In the cable installation company, installation engineers felt trapped rather than liberated by their task-related workload. Most employees at this contracting company were semi-skilled installation engineers. Until 1998, they had a mandatory six-day week, 'Monday to Saturday inclusive' specified in their contract, along with 'Hours of work: your hours of work are those required to carry out your duties to the satisfaction of the Company and as necessitated by the needs of the business'. This does not appear to leave much scope for employee flexibility.

Jack, who complained that he scarcely saw his children in the week while working for the company, said:

You'd get your jobs for the day allocated and go to the Stores at 7.30 to collect equipment – all non-productive time – then get to the job. 'Hits' can take up to two hours. The idea is that, if you average jobs out, they take around two to two-and-a-half hours and you do five or six a day – which makes a long day even when things go smoothly. It was quite normal to work for 60–80 hours a week, until nine or ten o'clock at night. Six days a week! You're permanently tired! On Sundays there are things to do at home and you're getting pressure at home because you're never there.

The onus is on the installers to be as fast and productive as possible, to maximise their earnings in an unstable situation where next week, they might be put on short time if there isn't enough business.

Trevor agreed. Now working for one of the biggest ICT companies, upon whom WideTec depends for contracts, he commented that telecoms WideTec is one of the better contractors in terms of the pay and conditions it offers employees. The sector, though, is highly competitive and even firms such as his current one were alleged to encourage the cutting of corners and exploitation of direct and sub-contracted employees.

'The risk just gets passed down', he said. 'My company puts tight constraints and penalties on WideTec, and they put the screws on their workers. In the end, health and safety are at risk and it becomes a vicious circle.'

Temporary working among operatives and production workers

Temporary employment at an establishment was often perceived as an effective 'way in' to more secure employment there. There were several cases where temps had been employed for an initial period and then taken on permanently by the company, and this could be a particularly beneficial way for the unemployed to access job opportunities. In such cases, temporary staff were generally taken on where the level of demand for a product or service was initially difficult to predict, and offered permanent contracts when demand levels stabilised.

In Cakefood, of the 30 most recent new recruits, approximately half had been working as temporary operatives at the factory. Because the plant was diversifying and had benefited from new investment by its parent company, extra staff were being recruited after major job losses during the late 1980s and early 1990s.

One man had been employed at the factory for five years as a temp before being offered a permanent contract two years ago. When he first started he commented that he was lucky if he got more than two five-hour shifts in a week, but gradually his hours had increased as the factory diversified.

However, temporary staff were often visibly separate from colleagues working alongside them on the production lines, for instance by wearing different coloured overalls from everyone else which marked them out as being 'different'. The prospect of being taken on permanently also has to be balanced against the precariousness of the temps' status and the irregularity they faced in their working hours.

Another man at Cakefood described how his colleague had been made redundant and came back to work as a temp at the factory a week later. The colleague found that he did not have the same routine as when he was a permanent employee, and could be 'stuck on nights' for two weeks and then shifted to afternoons with little notice, making it difficult to plan ahead.

Like some professionals, not all operative staff wanted to have a permanent contract. In many hotels, for example, casual staff employed on the hotel's register had refused permanent contracts because they were happy to maintain the control they had over their working hours and found that this way of working was convenient for them to combine their family commitments with employment. They tended to be women with children who wanted to be able to vary their working hours to suit their domestic responsibilities, yet remain fairly certain that they would be called in for a minimum number of hours per week. In many of the hotels, which relied heavily on these 'casual banks', two or three shifts per week were almost guaranteed – such as at Grand City Hotel.

Traditional seasonal working was found among the ultimate 'professional casuals' in this large five-star hotel in London. Here, highly experienced food service waiters were prepared to work long hours over the banqueting season, sometimes packaging together between 50 and 70 hours per week across 12 to 15 sessions at different hotels. Several of these had been working at the establishment for 20 years on a casual basis. Although they were paid by the session they could receive premiums for unsociable hours or particularly busy events and the tips they received (largely untaxed) were considerable. Such employees (most of them men) fulfilled a traditional 'male breadwinner' role but at the cost of onerous hours which were not particularly conducive to participatory parenthood. They were also uncovered by employment rights such as holiday and sick pay, although in cases of long-standing service sick pay was often provided at the discretion of the hotel management.

The disaggregated costs and benefits of different working arrangements and contractual relationships for operative and production workers are presented in Table 16.

Non-permanent workers and employment rights

Reduced employment rights such as limited or no access to sick pay and holiday pay were a major issue for temporary workers, who seldom had access to the same entitlements enjoyed by permanent employees at the time of the research shown by Table 17. For some non-permanent staff this was not a problem: highly qualified and experienced IT contractors were able to command rates more than sufficient to fund private provision for themselves and their families.

For many, however, reduced access to holiday and sick pay and limited availability of occupational pensions combined with

Table 16 The costs and benefits of different flexible working practices and contractual arrangements for operatives and production workers

Type of flexibility	Benefits	Costs
Permanent structured	**Food manufacturing and hotels** *Fixed shifts*: regular hours of work, predictability	**Food manufacturing and hotels** *Fixed shifts*: often encompassed unsociable hours *Rotating shifts:* can be physically and socially disruptive.
Permanent unstructured	**Food manufacturing** *Overtime*: shift premiums **Hotels** *Variable shifts*: ability to vary working hours to suit personal circumstances or financial needs, ability to match working hours to suit family or other non-work commitments	**Food manufacturing** *Overtime*: infringement upon non-work time, long hours, (sometimes) unpredictable and disruptive **Hotels** *Variable shifts*: irregular income and unpredictable hours, potentially leading to reduced entitlements to contributory benefit system
Temporary structured	**Food manufacturing** *Agency labour supply contract*: a 'way in' to the company's permanent workforce, relatively secure within terms of the contract	**Food manufacturing** *Agency labour supply contract*: generally engaged in lower grade work for less pay than permanent employees
Temporary unstructured	**Food manufacturing and hotel** *Zero-hours/casual contracts*: opportunity to access permanent employment within the organisation, opportunity to move in and out of the labour force	**Food manufacturing and hotel** *Zero-hours/casual contracts:* insecure employment, irregular working hours, lack of employment rights and employee benefits **Telecoms (cable installation)** *Zero-hours*: unpredictable hours and income from week to week: long hours or short-time working

Source: Institute for Employment Research.

Table 17 Employment benefits by contractual status

Benefits received	Permanent employees (%)	Fixed-term contract employees (%)	Other temporary employees (%)
Holiday pay	89	73	62
Sick pay	90	95	81
Pension contribution	81	50	43
Private health insurance	7	5	4

Source: Institute for Employment Research – 'Whose Flexibility?' employee survey.

temporary employment status led to increased insecurity and reliance on state benefits. Most of those employed on a series of short-term contracts or on a zero-hours basis were likely to be in low or unskilled jobs with limited access to the most basic employment rights and no access at all to employee benefits enjoyed by their permanent counterparts. In many of these jobs, especially those involving shift work or variable hours, temporary staff were not eligible for overtime premiums and therefore the potential to supplement their basic earnings from work was low.

For some non-permanent staff the unpredictability of working hours also meant unpredictable earnings. For many of the agency workers at Cakefood, for example, the number of hours they were allotted could vary from two shifts to five or six every week. A high proportion of these workers were low skilled with few qualifications and had been unable to find permanent work. The majority of them were either younger men with intermittent employment records or older men aged 40 or over who had been made redundant and could not secure alternative full-time, permanent work, for whom the impact of such intermittent employment was often a highly precarious household income.

In the hotels, casual staff tended to prefer this status because many of them were students working to top-up their grant and loans or women returners seeking to supplement the family income. While they did not have such a strong orientation towards permanent work, regular working hours remained very important given the need to balance work with study or family commitments. The so-called status of such 'casual' employees was often questionable in terms of employment law. Many of them – like the waiters at the Grand City Hotel – had built up several years of continuous service and subsequently they had access to employment rights such as holiday and sick pay entitlements (*pro rata*) which other 'casual' staff – those employed more sporadically, who did not have 13 weeks' continuous employment at the establishment – did not have. It is also likely that, for many, their earnings were not merely a 'top-up' but an essential component of the household income (cf. Purcell *et al.*, 1999). The intermittent employment histories and irregular working hours of such employees may also impact upon longer-term security as employees fail to accumulate National Insurance Contributions because of their short part-time hours or irregular employment records, limiting eligibility for many contributory benefits and leading to reduced state pension entitlement (McKnight *et al.*, 1998).

Those on non-permanent contracts felt substantially less secure: over a third were dissatisfied with their job security. The non-permanent employees who felt most secure were on fixed-term contracts, which were often on a renewable basis. Those who felt least secure were employed on a temporary basis directly by the establishment concerned. Such employees lacked both the limited security of a fixed-term contract and the support of being signed to an agency where, to an extent, responsibility for finding alternative employment could be transferred to the intermediary.

There was also a high degree of insecurity within the permanent workforce – approximately one-fifth of these employees expressed dissatisfaction with their job security: a finding reminiscent of trends revealed by another current JRF project (Burchell *et al.*, 1999) which found that degree of insecurity was based on likely consequences as well as likelihood of being made redundant. A breakdown of full-time insecure employees by sector reveals that the majority of them were employed in further education establishments. This is a sector where there has been a great deal of upheaval and organisational restructuring in recent years, including some industrial unrest, and clearly the growth of temporary and casual work among a formerly secure profession with attractive terms and conditions has impacted upon the morale of many lecturing staff regardless of their contractual status (Tebbutt and Marchington, 1997).

Conclusion

Table 18 gives an overview of the costs and benefits of different contractual relationships and flexible working patterns for employees. Permanent structured flexibility offered many benefits to staff where it was paired with an understanding attitude on the part of management towards employees having to meet family commitments. Where control of working time was dictated by management (in order to meet production schedules or a specific pattern of service delivery), clerical and operative staff preferred the predictability of set hours of work which allow them to plan ahead and arrange their non-work time.

As outlined in the case studies of NorBank and Bevfood, unpredictable or unstructured working hours were unpopular because even a few extra unplanned hours could cause disruption to employees' plans, particularly their child care arrangements. Variable working hours were only preferred by staff where they had the autonomy to decide when and indeed whether to work. Among management and professionals, flexi-time and annualised hours were beneficial in allowing them to achieve more of a balance between work and non-work time, but there remained a gravitation towards working long hours (frequently unpaid) as a sign of career commitment and to cope with heavy workloads, even in those organisations where flexible working time was offered.

The costs and benefits of different forms of contract varied greatly between sectors as organisational and labour market contexts had a

Table 18 Relative costs and benefits and types of flexibility for employees

	Structured flexibility	Unstructured flexibility
Permanent	**Costs** May involve having to work unsociable or non-standard hours May be difficult to get time off, particularly if working part-time **Benefits** Able to plan time ahead because of regularity of hours Scope to achieve a sensible balance between work and family commitments	**Costs** Unpredictable working hours Long working hours encroaching into non-work time **Benefits** Able to match working hours to varying workloads Greater autonomy over working hours helping to achieve a better balance between work and non-work time Premiums for working overtime
Unstructured flexibility	**Costs** Weak 'psychological contract' Limited access to employee benefits and employment rights Limited scope for career development and opportunities for progression **Benefits** An income maximisation strategy for employees with sought after skills and experience An effective 'way in' to an expanding organisation	**Costs** Very weak 'psychological contract' No access to employee benefits and employment rights High level of job insecurity Lack of 'inclusion' within the workplace No post-induction training or career development **Benefits** Control over workload to suit personal circumstances or financial need

Source: Institute for Employment Research.

strong influence on the acceptability or otherwise of non-permanent status. Among software personnel, particularly those working in telecoms, contracting was an aspiration rather than a disadvantage. For other groups of staff, particularly the lower skilled, being employed on a short-term contract resulted in more costs than benefits, unless they were in the position to be working at an expanding organisation where the likelihood of being 'promoted' to permanent status was strong. Ironically, in the case of many casual and zero-hours workers in hotels, we found that many preferred this arrangement, regarding their status not primarily as that of temporary workers but as part-timers, because of the regularity of work they received. Recent changes such as the EU Working Time Regulations will bring such employees into the scope of holiday and sick pay entitlements, which, at the time of research, many of them did not receive.

Altogether it is clear that the majority of the costs of flexible employment are borne predominantly by those in a weaker position in the labour market, either because of a lack of skills and qualifications which limit the kind of job opportunities they have available to them, or because of organisational restructuring which has jeopardised their employment security and subsequently eroded their bargaining power with employers.

7 Key findings

Employers' use of flexible employment contracts

The employers' use of flexible work contracts, looking at similarities and differences across sectors, assesses the relative impact of product and labour market pressures on employers' policies and practices. A number of different approaches adopted by employers were identified:

- In some establishments where organisations operated in highly competitive product markets for which labour costs were a substantial component of their prices – notably further education colleges and call centres in the banking and telecommunications industry and the cable-installation company – employers had clearly attempted to transfer the increasing risk attached to the product market to the employee where this was feasible.
- In situations of collective employee power, where trade unions had exerted pressure to protect permanent and full-time jobs, such as in the food manufacturing, further education and banking sectors, employers had pursued greater flexibility within permanent employment contracts, by the introduction of new contracts of employment requiring greater willingness to vary hours of work, annual hours working and the extension of 'standard' working hours to eliminate premium payments.
- Where employers had an equal opportunities commitment to family-friendly policies and also in situations of individual employee power where particular skills were at a premium – such as for highly skilled ICT staff in telecommunications – employers had introduced a more variable deployment of working time to attract and retain high quality employees.
- Some employers took an expedient response to product and labour market pressures as and when they arose, particularly in situations of labour scarcity. Most of the further education colleges and hotel and catering establishments provided examples of this. This was an identifiable strategy. Both preferred to employ a mixture of permanent and directly employed temporary staff, but used agencies and, in some cases, sub-contracting arrangements when faced with labour shortages which they could not meet directly from the labour market.

Employers' perceptions of the costs and benefits of employment flexibility

Employers recognised the benefits of building flexibility into the permanent contract of employment because it supplied them with a committed and loyal workforce that was able to adapt to fluctuations in demand.

- In the production worker context, the costs accrued because negotiation of new flexibilities often required time-consuming consultative processes. Employers, however, were convinced that the benefits outweighed the costs.

- In administrative, technical and professional occupations, a more informal type of flexibility tended to have developed where there was tacit agreement between employers and employees of reciprocal working time flexibility. Employees' occasional needs to, say, leave work early, would be agreed in implicit counterbalance to the expectation that the employee would stay late at some point to finish a piece of work.

Contracts of employment that were temporary or made for a highly tenuous relationship between employee and employer tended to suit firms at the lower end of the value added spectrum, or requiring low-skilled workers. Employers deploying, for instance, zero-hour contracts, were able to transfer a large part of the risk attached to demand for their products or services to the employee. If there was no work, employees were not employed. Tellingly, there was evidence that employers who had developed somewhat tenuous employment relationships with their employees but who were seeking to move up the value added ladder wanted to make the relationship between their staff and themselves more concrete, particularly in areas of skill shortages.

By and large, the more highly skilled employees were, the more likely it was that employers saw the costs of non-standard *contractual arrangements* as outweighing the benefits. They were more likely to offer non-standard *working arrangements*, or employee-friendly flexibility, to attract such staff to their permanent workforce.

- Fixed-term contracts were used where labour demand (or, in the case of further education, capacity to fund posts) was unpredictable, and as 'cautious recruitment'.
- Zero-hours contracts, where labour supply was plentiful, were seen to have benefits which outweighed the costs, but to be suitable for a limited range of posts.

Employees' perceptions of the costs and benefits of employment flexibility

The analysis of employee responses shows that occupation, degree of skill and, essentially, labour market power – whether deriving from such attributes or labour shortages – determine that costs outweigh the benefits for employees with 'non-standard' contractual relations or flexible working arrangements; and degree of structure in the flexibility was closely correlated with degree of satisfaction with working arrangements. Where staff had more influence over their hours through flexi-time or annual hours systems, there appeared to be higher levels of satisfaction with the organisation of working time and in particular the balance between work and home life. Flexi-time and job sharing for clerical staff were found in several of the FE colleges and telecoms companies, while, in the food manufacturing sector, office staff perceived such arrangements to be helpful in allowing them to meet their family commitments.

For those in higher level occupations, unstructured flexibility often entailed the willingness to work long hours 'as and when required' as part of the job; which countered equal opportunities commitments to 'family-friendly' flexibility in practice and raised important issues in terms of psychological well-being. This was particularly the case for permanent employees in further education and hospitality. However, in the food sector, there were signs of management desire to eliminate the long hours' culture in favour of 'working smarter' – partly to attract able younger recruits of both sexes.

Shift-working had been a traditional aspect of both hotel and food manufacturing sectors, although in very different forms, with a predominance of 'part-time' shifts in hotels slotted in to the working day at peak times, compared to mainly full-time shift patterns in the factories in order to cover 24 hour production schedules. In both these cases, the general trend was for structured flexibility from both full- and part-time staff, which enabled employees to plan how their work and outside commitments could be reconciled. Only where management expected changed hours at short notice did employees complain. Variable shifts and short-time working were particularly disliked.

The presence of more women within the food manufacturing companies had led to a less formally structured arrangement of working hours where overtime was concerned, and some companies were experimenting with the idea of introducing more part-time shifts into the production schedule in order to attract female employees and match them to production peaks. Such practices are commonplace within both the hotel and finance sectors, where the gendered labour supply was taken account of, with both structured flexibility and the informal flexibility sometimes required by parents built into custom and practice.

Temporary employment at an establishment was frequently perceived as an effective 'way in' to permanent employment there – and had been proved to be so. However, in some cases, staff who had been contractually employed on a non-permanent basis had in fact been employed as 'temps' for several years by the same company, leading to a degree of frustration and resentment. Several organisations were in the process of shifting such staff onto a more structured contractual footing (typically by offering them a fixed-term contract). There was concern that this may in effect erode some of their employment rights accrued through long-standing continuous service.

Employee perceptions of the costs and benefits of different forms of contract varied greatly according to subjective considerations. For example, among many software personnel, contracting was an aspiration rather than a disadvantage. For others, being employed on a short-term contract was deemed to result in many more costs than benefits, including limited opportunity for career progression, low morale, and reduced access to employee benefits (although recent legislation such as the EU Working Time Directive will improve the situation regarding holiday and sick pay entitlements for many).

Conclusions

The conclusions that emerge from the study are:

- Occupational groups tend to be affected differently by arrangements designed to facilitate employment flexibility. Managerial and clerical workers, particularly those with scarce expertise or skills, mainly experience a net benefit, whereas, for most manual and lower skilled workers, the costs appear to outweigh the benefits – flexibility means insecurity and unpredictability rather than an opportunity to achieve greater balance in their lives. Far from being family-friendly, low-skilled, part-time and temporary work and shift-working more often involve incursions into 'family time', particularly where the flexibility is unstructured.

- Flexible contracts of employment nevertheless allow certain groups of individuals to participate in the labour market who would otherwise be unable to do so – especially those where flexible arrangements are structured and predictable, as in fixed part-time hours, or where the employee has skills where they are able to decide on the pattern of intermittent employment, rather than simply being subject to employers' fluctuating labour requirements.
- Employers who had balanced the needs of employees for employment flexibility as well as their own requirement for labour force flexibility were likely to take a segmented approach to recruitment, seeking to match employees' needs in order to achieve workforce stability and/ or 'natural wastage turnover' as required. Thus some of the hotel and catering establishments sought to employ students and single parents at times convenient for both parties. The finance and food manufacturing employers tended to use temporary employment either as 'careful recruitment' where longer-term future demand was unpredictable or to target particular 'short-term' labour market populations who sought only temporary work.
- Employers accrue costs as well as benefits resulting from the application of highly flexible contracts, notably high labour turnover, absenteeism, and a weak psychological contract which can result in low commitment and poor employee performance. Several of the organisations which had used agency and temporary workers in the past, for example, further education colleges, hotels and call centres in the finance and telecommunications sectors, had been moving to minimise such use in the interests of improved employee performance and commitment.
- The costs of flexible contracts to the employee are particularly high where the application of good employment practices more broadly is not well developed.

The implications for employers and policy-makers

Highly flexible employment contracts clearly suit some groups at the margins of the labour market; for example, students who staff telephone help-lines or hotels for part-time or weekend shifts which fit in with their study commitments. Such transient workers are likely to form an increasing fraction of the workforce in response to changes in higher education funding. In other examples, colleges of further education provided piecework contracts that allowed people to pursue happily one or more careers, such as musicians supplementing their income with some teaching work. What is more important, perhaps, is to consider the impact of flexible contracts of employment on the mainstream labour force and on employment opportunities for socially excluded groups. In so far as employers can meet their staffing needs with fractional or casual employees, will they have any incentive to create more stable job opportunities which imply longer-term commitment to members of the workforce?

Perhaps it is not the degree of flexibility which should be focused on by policy-makers and stakeholders other than employers, so much as the terms and conditions of employment specified in the employment contract or practised through internal human resource policies. Of course, poorer terms and conditions of employment may well be related to highly flexible employment contracts – notably the limited application of employment rights legislation – but the study has also highlighted examples of companies that faced problems of absenteeism, low worker motivation and satisfaction despite their staff possessing permanent full-time contracts of employment. It also highlighted the fact that, on the whole, employers find it more efficient (and financially beneficial, in the long term) to employ the majority of their workers on permanent contracts and to offer them terms and conditions which nurture a high-trust psychological contract and workforce stability. Sennett (1998) has provided convincing evidence that even highly skilled and high status employees who benefit financially from purely task-related and transient contractual arrangements are likely to have a psychological contract with their temporary employers which is ultimately both personally and organisationally psychologically corrosive.

In the larger establishments, there was a recognition that human resource policy needed to value staff highly at all stages of the production or service process, although this did not always equate with offering a permanent contract of employment, as the examples from the banking industry testify. Even if a contract was for a specific period of time, emphasis was given to offering staff opportunities for development and mutually satisfactory terms and conditions of employment for the duration of the contract. This is clearly a more difficult ideal to achieve for small or insecure organisations operating in highly competitive product markets. It is perhaps not surprising that the case study organisations offering the most disadvantageous terms and conditions of employment to their workers were the two telecoms firms operating in highly competitive sub-sectors: WideTec and CallTec, both of which were dependent upon tendering for contracted work from client organisations – thus insecure organisations employing insecure workers (in fact, WideTec has been forced out of business since the completion of this research). The other sector characterised by employee discontent was FE, which reflected deterioration of contractual and working conditions in the face of funding reductions and future uncertainties. The key message is that coerced flexibility is unlikely to lead to organisational suppleness and, indeed, is probably impossible to achieve – whereas mutually agreed flexibility almost certainly reflects good organisational health and high trust relations.

In most of the case study establishments, there was definite evidence of core–periphery employment practices and awareness of the advantage of segmented recruitment among the employers interviewed, and to the extent that less highly skilled jobs can be fragmented without damage to productive or service quality – as in hospitality and retail part-time employment – there is likely to be an increase in flexible working, and decrease in job opportunities which provide for the full subsistence needs of incumbents. The challenge for employers and policy-makers in the immediate future will be to ensure that such jobs supplement rather than replace 'real jobs' and provide employee flexibility rather than reinforcing dependence on the family, the community and the State.

References

Atkinson, J. and Meager, N. (1986) *Changing Work Patterns: How Companies Achieve Flexibility to Meet New Needs*. London: National Economic Development Office

Beatson, M. (1995) *Labour Market Flexibility*, Employment Department Research Paper No. 48. Sheffield: Employment Department

Beck, U. (1992) *Risk Society: Towards a New Modernity*. London: Sage

Beechey, V. and Perkins, T. (1986) *A Matter of Hours: Women, Part Time Work and the Labour Market*. Cambridge: Polity Press

Burchell, B., Day, D., Hudson, M., Lapido, D., Mankelow, R., Nolan, J., Reed, H., Wichert, I. and Wilkinson, F. (1999) *Job Insecurity and Work Intensification: Flexibility and the Changing Boundaries of Work*. York: Joseph Rowntree Foundation

CAB (Citizens' Advice Bureau) (1997) *Flexibility Abused: A CAB Evidence Report on Employment Conditions in the Labour Market*. London: CAB

Casey, B., Metcalf, M. and Millward, N. (1997) *Employers' Use of Flexible Labour*. London: PSI

Cave, K. (1997a) 'Close to the core: zero-hours working surveyed', *Flexible Employment*, Vol. 2, No. 3, pp. 21–3

Cave, K. (1997b) 'Zero hours – the legal implications', *Flexible Working*, Vol. 2, No. 4, pp. 23–6

Colling, T. (1995) *From Hierarchy to Contract? Subcontracting and Employment in the Service Economy*. Warwick Papers in Industrial Relations, No. 52

Corfield Wright (1996) *Flexible Working Means Business*. London: Corfield Wright

Cousins, C. (1999) 'Changing regulatory frameworks and non-standard employment: a comparison of Germany, Spain, Sweden and the UK', in A. Felstead and N. Jewson (eds) *Global Trends in Flexible Labour*. Basingstoke: Macmillan Business

Crouch, C. (1996) 'Atavism and innovation: labour legislation and public policy since 1979 in political perspective', *Historical Studies in Industrial Relations*, No. 2, September, pp. 111–24

Cully, M., O'Reilly, A., Millward, N., Forth, J., Woodland, S., Dix, G. and Bryson, A. (1998) *The 1998 Workplace Employee Relations Survey: First Findings*. London: Department of Trade and Industry with the Economic and Social Research Council, Advisory, Conciliation, and Arbitration Service, and PSI

Daniel, W.W. (1987) *Workplace Industrial Relations and Technical Change*. London: F. Pinter

Dex, S. and McCullough, A. (1995) *Flexible Employment in Britain: A Statistical Analysis*. Manchester: Equal Opportunities Commission Research Series, No. 15

Felstead, A. and Jewson, N. (1999) *Global Trends in Flexible Labour*. Basingstoke: Macmillan Business

FRES (Federation of Recruitment and Employment Services Limited) (1998) *Recruitment Industry Survey 1997/8*. London: FRES

Gallie, D. (1998) *Restructuring the Employment Relationship*. Oxford: Oxford University Press.

Gallie D. and White, M. (1995) 'Employer policies, employee contracts and labour market structure', in J. Rubery and F. Wilkinson (eds) *Employer Strategy and the Labour Market.* Oxford: Oxford University Press

Gregg P. and Wadsworth, J. (1995) 'A short history of labour turnover, job tenure, and job security, 1975-93' *Oxford Review of Economic Policy*, Vol. 11, No. 1, pp. 73–90

Gregg, P. and Wadsworth, J. (1996) 'Mind the gap: the changing distribution of entry wages in Great Britain', Centre for Economic Performance Discussion Paper No. 303, London School of Economics and Political Science

Gregg, P., Knight, G. and Wadsworth, J. (1997) 'Heaven knows I'm miserable now: job insecurity in the British labour market', Centre for Economic Performance Preliminary Working Paper No. 892, London School of Economics and Political Science

Guest, D. and Conway, N. (1997) *Employee Motivation and the Psychological Contract.* Issues in People Management, No. 21. London: Institute of Personnel Development (IPD)

Hakim, C. (1990) 'Core and periphery in employers' workforce strategies: evidence from the 1987 ELUS survey', *Work, Employment and Society*, Vol. 4, No. 2, pp. 157–88

Hakim, C. (1996) *Key Issues in Women's Work.* London: Athlone

Handy, C. (1984) *The Future of Work.* Oxford: Blackwell

Harrison, B. (1994) *Lean and Mean: The Changing Landscape of Corporate Power in the Age of Flexibility.* New York: Basic Books

Harvey, M. (1999) 'Economies of time: a framework for analysing the restructuring of employment relations', in A. Felstead and N. Jewson (eds) *Global Trends in Flexible Labour.* Basingstoke: Macmillan Business

Heather, P., Rick, J., Atkinson, J. and Morris, S. (1996) 'Employers' use of temporary workers', *Labour Market Trends*, September, pp. 403–12

Hewitt, P. (1996) 'The place of part-time employment', in P. Meadows (ed.) *Work out – or Work in?* York: Joseph Rowntree Foundation

Hogarth, T. (1993) 'Worker support for organisational and technical change: workplace industrial relations in UK manufacturing', *Work Employment and Society*, Vol. 7, No. 2, pp. 189–212

Hörning, K., Gerhard, A. and Michailow, M. (1995) *Time Pioneers: Flexible Working Time and New Lifestyles.* Cambridge: Polity

Hospitality Training Foundation (1996) *Catering and Hospitality Industry: Key Facts and Figures.* London: HTF

Husbands, C. (1998) 'Job flexibility and variations in performance and motivations for longer-term part-time teaching auxiliaries at the London School of Economics and Political Science', *Work, Employment and Society*, Vol. 12, No. 1, pp. 121–44

Hutton, W. (1995) *The State We're In.* London: Jonathan Cape

IDS (1999) 'Students in employment. From casual to structural: students working through the college term', IDS Report 776, January, pp. 10–11

Industrial Society, The (1997) *Maximising Attendance – Managing Best Practice*, No. 22. Birmingham: The Industrial Society

Institute of Management (1996) *Flexibility on Fairness: A Survey of Managers' Attitudes to Part-time Employment and Part-time Employees*. Research Report. London: Institute of Management/Trade Union Congress

IPD (Institute for Personnel Development) (1997) *Managing Diversity: An IPD Position Paper.* London: IPD

Jenkins, C. and Sherman, B. (1979) *The Collapse of Work*. London: Eyre Methuen

Joseph Rowntree Foundation (1995) *Enquiry into Income and Wealth*. York: Joseph Rowntree Foundation

Kochan, T. and Osterman, P. (1994) *The Mutual Gains Enterprise*. Cambridge, MA: Harvard University Press

Kodz, J., Kersley, B., Strebler, M. and O'Regan, S. (1998) *Breaking the Long Hours Culture*, Report No. 352. Brighton: IES

Lester, T. (1995) 'Flexibility: myths and realities', *Human Resources*, September/October, pp. 24–32

Lewis, S. (1997) '"Family friendly" employment policies: a route to changing organizational culture or playing about at the margins?', *Gender, Work and Organisation*, Vol. 4, No. 1, pp. 13–23

Lindley, R. (1987) *New Forms and New Areas of Employment Growth*. Luxembourg: CEC

Marsh, P. (1996) 'Reconciling employment and family responsibilities: a European perspective', in S. Lewis and J. Lewis (eds) *The Work-Family Challenge*. London: Sage

McKnight, A., Elias, P. and Wilson, R. (1998) *Low Pay and the National Insurance System: A Statistical Picture.* Manchester: Equal Opportunities Commission.

Meadows, P. (ed.) (1996) *Work out – or Work in?* York: Joseph Rowntree Foundation

Millward N., Stevens, M., Smart, D. and Hawes, W.R. (1992) *Workplace Industrial Relations in Transition*. Aldershot: Dartmouth

Mintel (1996) *Employment Agencies: Market Size and Trends*. Mintel Marketing Intelligence, Report No. 100596

Moss, P. (1996) 'Reconciling employment and family responsibilities: a European perspective', in S. Lewis and J. Lewis (eds) *The Work–Family Challenge*. London: Sage

Office for National Statistics (1997) *Social Trends 27*. London: The Stationery Office

Piore, M. and Sabel, C. (1984) *The Second Industrial Divide: Possibilities for Prosperity*. New York: Basic Books

Procter, S., Rowlinson, M., McArdle, L., Hassard, J. and Forrester, P. (1994) 'Flexibility, politics and strategy: in defence of the model of the flexible firm', *Work, Employment and Society*, Vol. 8, No. 2, pp. 221–42

Purcell, J. (1996) 'Contingent workers and human resource strategy: rediscovering the core/periphery dimension', *Journal of Professional HRM*, No. 5, October, pp. 16–23

Purcell, K. (1998) 'Flexibility in employment', in R. Lindley and R.A. Wilson (eds) *Review of the Economy and Employment 1997/8: Labour Market Assessment*. Coventry: Institute for Employment Research, University of Warwick

Purcell, K. and Purcell, J. (1998) 'In-sourcing, outsourcing and the growth of contingent labour as evidence of flexible employment strategies', *European Journal of Work and Organisational Psychology*, Vol. 7, No. 1, pp. 39–59

Purcell, K., Simm, C. and McKnight, A. (1999) *The Lower Earnings Limit in Practice: Part-time Employment in the Hotel and Catering Industry*. Manchester: Equal Opportunities Commission

Rajan, A., Eupen, P. and Jaspers, A. (1996) *Britain's Flexible Labour Market – What Next?* Tunbridge Wells: CREATE/DfEE

Robinson, P. (1999) 'Explaining the relationship between flexible employment and labour market regulation', in A. Felstead and N. Jewson (eds) *Global Trends in Flexible Labour*. Basingstoke: Macmillan Business

Seabrook, J. (1988) *The Leisure Society*. Oxford: Blackwell

Sennett, R. (1998) *The Corrosion of Character: The Personal Consequences of Work in the New Capitalism*. London and New York: W.W. Norton and Company

Siebert, S. (1999) *Company Recruitment Policies: Implications for Production Workers*. York: Joseph Rowntree Foundation

Sly, F. and Stillwell, D. (1997) 'Temporary workers in Great Britain', *Labour Market Trends*, Vol. 105, No. 9, September, pp. 347–54

Streeck, W. (1987) 'The uncertainties of management and the management of uncertainties', *Work, Employment and Society*, Vol. 1, No. 3, pp. 281–308

Tebbutt, M. and Marchington, M. (1997) 'Look before you speak: gossip and the insecure workplace', *Work Employment and Society*, Vol. 11, No. 4, pp. 713–35

TUC (Trades Union Congress) (1998) *The Time of Our Lives: A TUC Report on Working Hours and Flexibility*. London: TUC

Watson, G. (1994) 'The flexible workforce and patterns of working hours in the UK', *Employment Gazette*, Vol. 102, No. 7, July, pp. 77–84

Watson, G. and Fothergill, B. (1993) 'Part-time employment and attitudes to part-time work', *Employment Gazette*, Vol. 101, No. 5, pp. 213–20

White, M. (1996) 'The labour market and risk', in P. Meadows (ed.) *Work out – or Work in?* York: Joseph Rowntree Foundation

White, M. and Forth, J. (1998) *Pathways Through Unemployment – the Effects of a Flexible Labour Market*. York: Joseph Rowntree Foundation

White, M. and Gallie, D. (1995) 'Employer policies and individual life chances', in J. Rubery and F. Wilkinson *Employment Strategy and the Labour Market*. Oxford: Oxford University Press

Wood, S. (ed.) (1989) *The Transformation of Work? Skill, Flexibility and the Labour Process*. London: Unwin Hyman

Titles available in the *Work and Opportunity* series:

Making work pay: Lone mothers, employment and well-being

Alex Bryson, Reuben Ford and Michael White

This study tracks a sample of lone mothers over five years to find out what works in moving them off benefit, and what really makes a difference in easing hardship.

£11.95

Bridges from benefit to work: A review

Karen Gardiner

An innovative study of 42 welfare-to-work initiatives, assessing which give best value for money, how many people they help, and what the level of take-up is.

£11.95

Combining work and welfare

Jane Millar, Steven Webb and Martin Kemp

An exploration of key questions surrounding in-work benefits, and the likely impact of the national minimum wage.

£11.95

Lone mothers moving in and out of benefits

Michael Noble, George Smith and Sin Yi Cheung

This study analyses how and why lone mothers move between income support and in-work benefits, and considers current and future policy directions.

£11.95

Pathways through unemployment: The effects of a flexible labour market

Michael White and John Forth

A study of the effects and long-term consequences of flexible forms of work – particularly the part-time, self-employed and temporary jobs often taken up by unemployed people.

£11.95

Local responses to long-term unemployment

Mike Campbell with Ian Sanderson and Fiona Walton

A review of research to date on how to reconnect the long-term unemployed to the labour market.

£12.95

Company recruitment policies: Implications for production workers

Stanley Siebert

This study explores whether increased regulation of the labour market has an impact on hiring standards, screening out less qualified workers and so reducing their job opportunities.

£12.95

Young men, the job market and gendered work

Trefor Lloyd

A study of whether young men are being adequately prepared for the contemporary workplace, and whether their, or others', gender assumptions are affecting their opportunities.

£10.95

Back to work: Local action on unemployment

Ian Sanderson with Fiona Walton and Mike Campbell

This report complements *Local responses to long-term unemployment* (above), presenting detailed case-study research into what local action is effective in getting people into work.

£13.95

Ending exclusion: Employment and training schemes for homeless young people

Geoffrey Randall and Susan Brown

An evaluation of the particular difficulties in finding work faced by this group, and an assessment of the impact of a range of projects designed to assist them.

£13.95

Job insecurity and work intensification: Flexibility and the changing boundaries of work

Brendan J. Burchell, Diana Day, Maria Hudson, David Ladipo, Roy Mankelow, Jane P. Nolan, Hannah Reed, Ines C. Wichert and Frank Wilkinson

An exploration into the effect of job insecurity on the social, physical and psychological well-being of employees.

£13.95

Whose flexibility? The costs and benefits of 'non-standard' working arrangements and contractual relations

Kate Purcell, Terence Hogarth and Claire Simm

Drawing on the experience of a range of industries and organisations, the report analyses the economic, operational and social effects of flexible employment practices.

£13.95

Further reports from this series will be published throughout 1999 and 2000.

All these reports are available from: York Publishing Services Ltd, 64 Hallfield Road, Layerthorpe, York YO31 7ZQ (Tel: 01904 430033; Fax: 01904 430868; e-mail: orders@yps.ymn.co.uk). Please include £2.00 post & packing per order.